"It is not enough to have met a word in the dictionary and to have experienced unpleasant adventures with it in the study of grammar. A word has a soul, and we must learn how to attain insight into its life."

Abraham Heschel, *Man's Quest for God*

Books by Skip Moen

Words to Lead By

Jesus Said to Her

God, Time and the Limits of Omniscience

Spiritual Restoration, Vol. 1

The Lucky Life

Spiritual Restoration, Vol. 2

Guardian Angel

Spiritual Restoration, Vol. 3

Cover Artwork by Donna Dozier

Cross
Word
Puzzles

A Brief Examination of the Meaning of the Cross from a Hebraic Perspective

By Skip Moen, D. Phil.

Acknowledgements

This study would not have been written were it not for the interaction between Mr. Robert Murray and myself. His tireless research of the texts crucial to understanding the Christian point of view were extremely helpful. Thank you, Bob.

In addition, I am very grateful for the work of Donna Dozier who not only proofread the document but provided a stunning cover for the book.

Of course, enthusiastic participants from the readership of *At God's Table* encouraged me to convert a single lecture into a scholarly study. Their support made all this a reality. In particular, Luzette Wessels of Kroonstad, South Africa, never let me put the work on the shelf and forget about it.

Finally, my wife Rosanne put up with endless hours of travel and absence as I flew around the world discussing and refining these ideas. She is truly my *'ezer kenegdo*. Nothing is accomplished without her.

Skip Moen
Montverde, 2013

Table of Contents

Introduction

Jesus died on the cross the forgiveness of sins.

This claim seems so abundantly clear to Christians that anyone who dares to question this tenet of the faith is quickly dismissed as a heretic. However, what seems obvious is often based on presupposition rather than evidence. For example, we continue to use the Euclidian geometric premise of a flat plane when we construct buildings even though scientists know that the earth is not flat and the real geometry must be of a curved surface. But Euclid works, so we keep him around. Assumptions often govern our thinking and prevent us from noticing anomalies. The same can be said of the Christian idea of atonement. For example, Wikipedia's very brief review of "Atonement in Christianity" cites four distinct understandings of the term *within* Christianity, not to mention the significant differences between the Jewish understanding of atonement and any of the Christian views. This should give us pause. If there is no uniform doctrine of atonement within the Church, why are we so resolutely convinced that atonement must be tied to the event of the cross? If Judaism does not view atonement as a "cross" event, how does atonement occur in Jewish thought; and why hasn't this view been transferred to Christian theology? And finally, where did the idea that Christ died on the cross for the forgiveness of sins come from? Who was the first to proclaim this connection, and how was it developed?

Religious readers may find such an examination unsettling. There is hardly a more fundamental belief of the contemporary evangelical church than the affirmation that Jesus died on the cross for my sins. In fact, this religious declaration is so universally accepted by the majority of evangelicals that it results in posters like the one I found in a church in Virginia. It read, "For God so loved the world that He gave is only begotten Son to die on the cross for the forgiveness of sin. – John 3:16." As I pointed out to the audience that evening, John 3:16 does not actually say anything like this. It does not mention the cross or forgiveness or sin. Those ideas were imported into the text from theological assumptions and then asserted as if the sacred text included them. The fact that no one objected to the religious poster, a poster widely sold across America, only serves to point out how little the religious community cares about what the Bible *actually* says. As long as the religious environment endorses what is assumed to be true, the words of the text don't really seem to matter.

My view is quite different. I believe that the words of the text are of ultimate importance. If Scripture does not support the claim, then the claim is false; if it does support the claim, then it is true; but there can be no waffling on this. A claim made without adequate Scriptural justification may fit the current religious belief system, but that does not make it biblically true. In my view, the claim that Jesus died on the cross for the forgiveness of sins is such a claim. It has been repeated so many times that it is now considered self-evident; but upon examination, I hope to show that it is not

2

historically accurate, culturally understandable or biblically supported.

Let me quickly add this: my rejection of the idea that the death on the cross was the place of atonement for sin does *not* mean that I reject the historical fact of the crucifixion *nor* does it mean that I do not think the event on the cross was the watershed event of human history. I believe that what was accomplished on the cross is the most important sign of God's redemptive purposes in all creation. I just don't believe that it has anything to do with forgiveness – as I hope to prove.

The investigation of the meaning of the cross must begin in the culture and historical period of the actual event. What Abelard taught about the cross, what Luther wrote about the cross, what Calvin found in exegesis about the cross are all far less important than answering the simple question, "What would a Jewish disciple of Yeshua think about the cross?" After all, nearly all of the original followers of the Jewish Messiah were *Jewish*. That means their religious perspective about this event would have been a function of their *Jewish* culture and theology. That they became advocates of Yeshua as the Messiah means that they accepted the cross as integral to their religious views, but that does not mean that they accepted any of the *Christian* conceptions of cross-atonement. Until we understand what the cross meant to these first believers, we will not know how to interpret the meaning of the cross in Scripture because Scripture is not a record of what the *Church* thinks about the cross; it is a record of what the earliest *Jewish* followers thought about the cross. The Christian interpretation comes later and, hopefully, is not at odds with what the authors of the New Testament actually believed. Hopefully.

We will see.

Chapter One

Christian Assumptions

No biblical scholar seriously doubts that Yeshua from Nazareth ("Jesus" in Christian parlance) died on the cross, executed as a criminal by the Roman procurator of Israel, sometime between 29AD and 33AD. It isn't his death that causes the controversy; it is the claim that He rose from the dead by the power of God. Conservative Christian believers have argued for decades that the evidence for the resurrection is a compelling justification for the claim that Yeshua is divine. Those who disagree with the Christian claim that "Jesus is God in the flesh" do not argue over the crucifixion; they argue over the resurrection. After all, Rome littered the landscape with crucified bodies. The unique claim of Christianity is not that Yeshua died; it is that Yeshua lives!

This leads Christians to quickly pass over their established truism, "Jesus died on the cross for the forgiveness of sins." Since they are most interested in getting to the next step of the declaration, "and He lives today because God raised Him from the dead," they don't pay too much attention to the details of the crucifixion other than to note its terrible physical suffering and its fulfillment of prophecy. In other words, the crucifixion is but a necessary precondition of the resurrection. It deserves its place in the passion of the Christ, but the real story is the story of Easter Sunday morning, not Friday afternoon.

Unfortunately, the focus on the resurrection causes Christians to overlook some oddities about the relationship between sacrifice and crucifixion. Overlooking these anomalies helps drive a wedge between a Jewish appreciation of the events of that particular Passover season and the Christian interpretation of those events. But the anomalies are worth serious investigation because the historical fact is that most believers in the first century were *Jewish*. If the events of that particular Passover didn't make sense to them *within the culture of Judaism in the first century*, then they would not have embraced Yeshua as the *Jewish* Messiah. Christians today seem to forget that Paul's letters were not in circulation when Yeshua hung on the cross. The gospel accounts were not written when these things happened. The only interpretive tool available for the people who witnessed these events was the Tanakh, understood within the culture of Judaism. If the cross didn't make sense *in that setting*, then those early Jewish believers would have rejected Yeshua as Messiah; but they didn't. That means they understood what happened on the cross from a Jewish perspective.

Christian believers today may bristle at the idea that the cross and the claims associated with it need to be understood within a Jewish context. They may claim that Jews who embraced the "true meaning" of the cross (i.e., the cross is the vehicle by which God reconciled the sinful world to Himself) *converted* to Christianity and therefore it is not necessary to understand these events *as Jewish*. They might claim that these events are what they are because they are *Christian*, not Jewish, and those who accepted them in the first century became Christians.

The problem with this explanation is that it just isn't true. It is popular, no doubt. Certainly virtually all Christians advocate this view. But that doesn't make it historically accurate. The overwhelming evidence from the text of the New Testament and the claims of its authors and characters, is that the earliest believers were Jewish and *remained Jewish* in their rituals, practices and conformity to Torah. While Christian apologists have tried to make the case that Jews *converted* to Christianity and thus initiated the new religion in the first century, there is no textual or historical evidence to support this. This claim is purely theological. It supports supersessionism; but it deliberately misreads the actual historical account.[1] It even requires an anachronistic reinterpretation of the very words of the witnesses as recorded in the New Testament.[2]

---

[1] A significant number of scholars have rejected the idea that Jews converted to Christianity during the New Testament period. These scholars point out that Christianity developed its self-identity in opposition to Judaism during the period from approximately 200AD to 400AD. There is evidence that even as late as 400AD Messianic communities were still following the Torah as a basis for ritual and practice. See Eisenbaum, Gager, Young, Bennett, Lancaster, Soulen, Hegg, Dacy, Becker, Reed.

[2] Consider the reinterpretation of Paul's claim in Acts 24:14-16. In his own words, Paul claims to serve God as a member of a so-called sect of *Judaism*, "believing everything that is in accordance with the Law, and that is written in the Prophets." He goes on the say that he maintains a blameless conscience before God and men. If we take Paul at his word, he clearly states that he remains Torah-observant, but innumerable Christian commentators ignore the plain meaning of his words, especially concerning his declaration that he keeps the

7

Therefore, we need to ask, "What would the cross have meant to the first century Jewish believer?" We can draw our conclusions from the text of the New Testament because all of the authors of the New Testament were either Jewish or proselytes to Judaism. Unless we find reasonable explanations for the *meaning* of the cross within a Jewish frame of reference, we simply won't understand how these early believers were able to accept this event as a sign that Yeshua was the Jewish Messiah. The question is not, "Did Yeshua die on the cross?" The question is "What does it mean?" As one theology professor used to say, "If you don't know what the author meant, you don't know what the text means."

"Law" because they have accepted a prior theological division between law and grace. Either Paul is lying or these commentators are deliberately ignoring what Paul actually said. See further Paul's statement in Philippians 3:5.

8

Noticing What's Odd

"The difference between fiction and reality is that fiction has to make sense."

Christians have asserted that Jesus died on the cross for the forgiveness of sins. This unexamined statement lies near to the heart of the Christian message, but because it is so much a part of Christian thinking, it rarely receives close scrutiny. It is *dogma*, not reality. It helps Christianity make sense. But when we examine the claim in the light of the first century audience and Scripture itself, it almost appears as fiction.

I do not mean to say that Yeshua didn't die on the cross. I am convinced that He did. What I mean is that the connection between His death on the cross and the forgiveness of Sin is not quite as firm as Christians would like to believe. Let's start examining this connection by noticing that Yeshua's death on the cross does *not* meet the requirements in the Tanakh for a sacrifice for sin. This step in our inquiry is important because all of the earliest interpreters of the meaning of this event were Jewish, and therefore, they knew what forgiveness of sins meant within the Jewish framework. Our examination must begin with the question, "How is atonement (forgiveness of sins) accomplished in the Jewish context?" Scripture tells us what the requirements must be. A sacrifice must be made at the altar. The blood must be sprinkled. The slaughter must be carried out in specific ways. Leviticus chapter 5 specifies these requirements:

1. The sin must be confessed (Lev. 5:5)
2. A guilt offering must be presented before the Lord (Lev. 5:6)
3. The guilt offering must be a female sheep, a lamb or a goat (Lev. 5:6)
4. The *priest* must make atonement on behalf of the sinner (Lev. 5:6, 8)
5. If the sinner cannot afford a lamb, then he may substitute two turtledoves or two pigeons, one for a sin offering and one for a burnt offering (Lev. 5:7)
6. The priest must sprinkle some of the blood on the offering on the side of the altar; the rest must be drained out on the base of the altar (Lev. 5:9)
7. If the sinner has insufficient means to afford two turtledoves or two pigeons, then he must bring a tenth of an ephah of fine flour (Lev. 5:11)
8. The flour must be offered by the priest (Lev. 5:13)

We must take note of some further requirements and complications:

1. If an animal is presented as a sacrifice, it must be unblemished
2. The priest must be from the Levitical order
3. On Yom Kippur, the great day of atonement, the sacrificial animal is *not* killed (Lev. 16:10, 21-22)
4. The Passover celebration (the event associated with Yeshua's death) is not recognized as an atonement event
5. Scripture specifically states that one man cannot die in atonement for another (Deuteronomy 24:16, Jeremiah 31:30)

Finally, as we see in Leviticus 5, there are alternatives for atonement. Blood sacrifice is *not* always required. For example, Numbers 16:46-47 allows incense to be used to make atonement for the people. Exodus 30:15-16 allows the payment of monetary funds to provide atonement when it is given for the service of the Tabernacle. Furthermore, of course, all of the requirements concerning atonement are for *unintentional* sins.

Atonement in the Tanakh can also be achieved by repayment and restitution, often with additional penalties attached. As we have seen, the provisions for atonement consider the economic condition of the supplicant. In the extreme case, even fine flour can be used as a sacrifice for the sin offering. Perhaps the ultimate example of forgiveness and atonement without the customary Levitical sacrifices is to be found in 1 Kings 8:46-50. At the dedication of the Temple, Solomon prays that God's anger may be diverted from a deserving, disobedient people "if they return to You with all their heart and with all their soul." In this instance, when the people are held captive in a land where there is no Temple, what is required is not sacrifices by the Levitical priests at the Temple, but rather repentance and supplication, confession and a plea for mercy. Solomon's instructions do not include even a hint at the usual Levitical order.

There are other biblical difficulties with the idea that atonement, especially substitutionary blood sacrifice atonement, is required to restore fellowship with God. Micah recounts God's own words about what is required in order to restore fellowship, and there is no mention of a substitutionary death among the three things Micah reveals (cf. Micah 6:8). Furthermore, Isaiah speaks on God's behalf (Isaiah 40:2) claiming that iniquity is removed because the people have suffered twice over. Again, there is no concept of substitutionary atonement present here. The suffering of the people *is the atonement*.

All of these considerations are part of the Hebraic/Jewish background of the first century. They cause us to ask with renewed scrutiny, "Does the substitutionary death of Yeshua produce forgiveness?" The writers of the New Testament answer, "Yes," but exactly how that is accomplished isn't quite so clear. The claim that Yeshua's death *on the cross* is the *only* way forgiveness is accomplished seems to ignore a significant portion of Scripture that would have been quite apparent to a Jewish audience.

Why is all this history important? An observant Jew in the first century would certainly know what was required for the forgiveness of sin. He would know the wide variety of sin sacrifices provided in the Tanakh. He would know that some sacrifices made no mention of blood. Furthermore, he would know that there was even a provision for atonement *without* the Levitical requirement. All of this would stand in stark contrast to the claim that Yeshua's death on the cross was the *only* sacrifice for sin.

As if that were not enough to cause us some cognitive dissonance, two New Testament authors tell us that the Lamb was slain *before* the foundation of the world and a third author tells us that the sacrifice was made in a Temple "not built with human hands." So according to the New Testament text itself, Yeshua's sacrifice, the preeminent sacrifice that provides forgiveness for sins, occurred before David, before Abraham and before Adam. This implies that there is no distinction between "Old Testament" sacrifice and "New Testament" grace. They are one and the same. If the critical sacrifice occurred *before* the foundation of the world, then Yeshua's sacrifice was already in place when Adam sinned. The claim that Old Testament righteousness is based on "works" but New Testament righteousness is based on "grace" is simply false. If the New Testament authors acknowledge that the essential sacrifice performed by Yeshua happened before the world was created, then it certainly was in effect at the time of Adam and Abraham; but if this is true, then what happened on the cross? We will have to examine all the elements of these claims before we can reach a conclusion that could have been acknowledged by Jewish believers in the first century.

Nicodemus and Moses

The typical assertion, "Jesus died on the cross for the forgiveness of sins" assumes that the event at Calvary established the means of forgiveness. But Yeshua Himself suggests another interpretation. Speaking to Nicodemus, Yeshua pointed toward Moses lifting up the serpent in the wilderness (Numbers 21:9) as an explanatory model. He directs us to look toward an ancient typology found in an event in the wilderness. Consider the context of Yeshua's dialogue with Nicodemus. "No one has ascended into heaven, but He who descended from heaven" opens the discussion. This is not about forgiveness. It is about power and glory. Only the One who comes down has the right to go back up. Origin determines authority. How will men know that this claim is true? They will see the sign of Moses, says Yeshua. They will see the power and glory of the Son of Man lifted up, both on the cross and in the ascension. Yeshua points Nicodemus to the event in the wilderness when Moses lifted up the copper snake. There is no doubt that Yeshua refers to this event as an explanation of the cross and the ascension (see John 3:14). But what does this odd story of the Israelites in the wilderness mean and why would He refer to it?

John's gospel uses the Greek verbs *hypsoo* and *dei* (must be lifted up). The first verb means both "to lift up" and "to exalt." In the LXX (Septuagint) it is often used for the exaltation of God (e.g., Isaiah 52:13). The word shows up in John 3:14, 8:28 and 12:32 as descriptions of the exalted Christ. To be lifted up on the cross is a sign of exaltation *and of death*.

Several Targums (rabbinic expansions and explanations of the Tanakh) suggest that this passage is related to the curse in Genesis 3:14. Archeological evidence suggests that copper (not bronze) snakes were part of the pagan religious iconography in the area, including Egypt. There is also a word play in Hebrew in the Numbers 21 passage. Moses makes a *nehash nehoshet*, the first word meaning "snake" and the second "copper." Rabbinic tradition teaches that YHWH did not simply remove this plague as He did in Egypt because, unlike the plagues of Egypt, this is a test of obedience. Only those who *looked* upon the icon were healed. This event becomes a symbol of faith in the word of the Lord and in His servant's action. The Hebrew verb used here (*sum*) has a variety of meanings and is frequently associated with YHWH. Among its umbrella of meanings are "to appoint, to set aside for a special purpose, to assign something, to establish a new relationship, and to bring about a change." Do you suppose that Yeshua wasn't aware of these meanings when He pointed Nicodemus toward this story? As a superb rabbi, wouldn't you expect Him to ask His student (Nicodemus) to discover the deeper truth in this story by examining it carefully? Wouldn't a word play on the multiple definitions fit rabbinic teaching?

What conclusions can we draw that assist us in understanding Yeshua's clue? First we find that once again YHWH uses something from familiar paganism to reverse the pagan belief. The children of Abraham would have been familiar with the winged Egyptian uraeus (the cobra) as a symbol of royalty, associated with the sun god and many other deities. Furthermore, this symbol was worn on the headdress as a *protective* icon. Now imagine that Moses fashions such a symbol, not as homage to the Egyptian gods but as a sign of healing and protection from the One true God. What would this mean to the Israelites? Wouldn't they see that one more Egyptian icon now falls under the power of YHWH? Wouldn't they recognize that true protection comes only *through* the efficacy of the Lord even if the icon once represented a pagan practice? In other words, the copper snake transforms prior idolatry into a standard of the Holy One of Israel. Life, death and healing are found, not in the representations of men, but in the standard lifted up by God.

Notice the parallel motifs in the first century. Roman crucifixion was the ultimate symbol of power over life. Crucifixion was the most brutal, most torturous, most cruel form of execution the Romans could devise. If there were ever a symbol of *death*, the cross was it. Now Yeshua does what Moses did in the wilderness. He transforms a symbolic representation of pagan control over life into a vehicle of healing through the One true God. The idolatry of Rome is converted into a sign of YHWH's sovereignty, just as the idolatry of Egypt was converted into a sign of YHWH's healing. And in both cases, the recipient must *look upon* that pagan symbol and *see* something new; not a sign of the power of Man's gods but a sign of the authority of Israel's God.

Perhaps Yeshua goes to the cross in order to establish God's final authority over the real enemy – death. If the sacrifice for forgiveness is accomplished before the world's foundation according to John, Peter and the author of Hebrews, then the cross represents God's victory over every form of idolatry holding men captive by the threat of death. "It is accomplished," takes on far greater meaning. Yeshua seems to imply that the cross is the gateway of the return of the heavenly kingdom. It is the final statement of "Thy will be done on earth as it is in heaven." Death is the vehicle that transports the Son of Man from earthly Messiah to coming King.

The text continues. "Whoever believes in Him may have eternal life." When the Son of Man is lifted up, those who believe acquire eternal life. Believe what? Obviously, not simply the fact that He is lifted up. Every crucified man was lifted up. What a witness must believe is that this is the sign of Yeshua's exaltation as Lord and Ruler. A witness must believe that Yeshua now reigns over all the earth. And this means that Yeshua rules over *me*! Notice that Yeshua does not say, "Those who believe will have forgiveness of their sins." Yeshua's statement focuses on overcoming the *result* of disobedience, not on the removal of the guilt of disobedience. When He is lifted up, those who believe will *live*! The obvious implication is that they will not *die*. Life and death are the issues here. The importance of the cross isn't about forgiveness. It's about power and authority. Who controls life and death? Where the world sees defeat, God sees victory! Through death He becomes Ruler and Lord of *life*! In this act, death is completely transformed, from a power that holds sway over any real meaning in life to a sign of the ultimate supremacy of the Lord's anointed. On the cross, death dies!

It is important to notice that Yeshua does *not* point to the resurrection. He doesn't say, "And when you see me live again after dying on the cross." He says that the sign of the cross is his *death* on the cross. Whatever He has in mind in this statement to Nicodemus, it doesn't seem to depend on the resurrection that follows His death. The meaning is to be found in the analogy with Moses in the wilderness, not in the sign of Jonah.

We have discovered that being lifted up is about exultation, not about forgiveness. But we need to pay even more attention to the context of both events, the image of the serpent lifted up in the wilderness and the Son of Man lifted up on the cross. There is more here than just this insight about exultation.

Consider the conversation with Nicodemus. Yeshua outlines what it means to be generated by the Spirit from above (usually translated inaccurately as "born again"). In this context, Yeshua hints at a verse from Deuteronomy (30:12).[3] When Moses speaks these words to the people, he is justifying the plain and simple truth of Torah. Torah is "not too hard and not too far off," says Moses. It is unnecessary for someone to *ascend to heaven* and bring Torah back to earth. God has given His instructions in plain language. This claim

---

[3] It is not in the heavens, to say, 'Who shall ascend into the heavens for us, and bring it to us, and cause us to hear it, so that we do it?'" Deuteronomy 30:12 ISR

18

would have been quite startling to ancient near-Eastern cultures because it was commonly believed that even though the gods *did* have demands, they did *not* reveal those demands to human beings. Consequently, human beings were operating in the dark. For YHWH to clearly reveal what He expected was singularly important. Basically, this means that *there are no excuses* for disobedience.

Notice how Yeshua uses the implications from Moses. No one has ascended, as Moses points out, but *one has descended*. This is essentially a claim of divinity. Yeshua is saying that He is the equivalent of Torah. Just as Torah came down from YHWH for the instruction and edification of the people, so Yeshua has come down to demonstrate the *living* Torah among YHWH's people. Nicodemus could hardly have missed the point.

This is the context of Yeshua's use of Numbers 21:9 (lifting up the serpent). In other words, Yeshua uses the idea of being lifted up as a sign of *authority*, not forgiveness. Once we remove the "born again" mistranslation, this conversation with Nicodemus reveals itself as a teaching about Yeshua's role as the living Torah, "the way, the truth and the life" of God's people. To be generated from above (as John 3:3 actually says) is to accept the authority of Yeshua as the final elaboration of Torah. Yeshua is not the *end* of Torah but rather the *full disclosure* of Torah as seen in the *exultation* of the Son.

The Hebrew word behind this conversation helps us clarify the meaning. That word is *rum*, found in Exodus 17:11 and Numbers 20:11. We know the context of Numbers 21:9, but consider the context of the other two verses. The first is about Moses lifting up his hands during battle. When his staff, lifted by his hands, was held high, Israel prevailed. When his staff fell, Israel did not prevail. Eventually Aaron and Joshua helped Moses hold up the staff. The second account concerns Moses lifting up his hand (staff) to strike the rock. These three events in the wilderness are all tied together with the word *rum*. Do you imagine that Nicodemus didn't know the associations with *rum* when Yeshua used this word in regard to the incident with the serpents? In every case, the event is about a display of *power*. Yeshua makes the connection when He uses the word *rum* to describe what happened with Moses and the serpent. If you were Nicodemus and you heard Yeshua use the Hebrew *rum* when describing *Himself*, what would you conclude – that He was offering forgiveness to the Gentiles – or would you see the connection to *divine exultation*?

In the conversation with Nicodemus, Yeshua says that He must be "lifted up" just as Moses lifted up the serpent in the wilderness. This appears to be a midrash – the application of a story from a different context in order to explain or amplify the meaning in another context. In order to understand what is happening on the cross, we are told to look at the event of the serpent on the pole. The Hebrew verb *rum* ("lift up") is found in other wilderness stories (e.g., Exodus 17:11) but it *isn't* found in Numbers 21:9, the story of the snake on the stick. That doesn't prevent Yeshua from using the verb to describe what Moses did. Translating the Greek text of John's gospel back into the spoken Hebrew of Yeshua, it is clear the Yeshua employs *rum* in order to point us toward Moses' action. This is midrash, a look at one context applied to another context. We are supposed to see the same action in both events.

Nearly sixty years of theological reflection on the meaning of the events in the life of Yeshua had passed by the time John wrote his gospel account. Perhaps that's why John begins his account with a deliberate allusion to Genesis. John's perspective is neither Jewish nor Gentile. John is interested in the *cosmic* implications of the good news. So John's vocabulary pushes us toward a much larger scale, a view of the impact of the incarnation on the entire creation. In the commentary on the conversation with Nicodemus,[4] John focuses the reader's attention on God's love for the *kosmos*. The real reason for the gift of the Son is the reconciliation of *all creation*. Paul echoes the same cosmic orientation when he says that the whole creation "has been groaning together in the pains of childbirth until now."[5] What is at stake is not simply the means of forgiveness for men. What is at stake is the reconciliation of the entire creation. What happens on the cross is far more significant than an altar sacrifice required for forgiveness. What happens on the cross is the final victory over an enemy that has held the *kosmos* captive since

---

[4] In spite of the typical indication in English Bibles that Yeshua spoke the words of John 3:16, scholars find it quite unlikely that these are the words of the Messiah. The context suggests that there are John's *commentary* on the implications of the prior conversation between Nicodemus and Yeshua. Of course, this doesn't make the words any less true.
[5] Romans 8:22 ESV

Genesis 3. The author of the book of Hebrews puts it like this:

> Since therefore the children share in flesh and blood, he himself partook of the same things, that through death he might destroy the one who has the power of death, that is, the devil, and deliver all those who through fear of death were subject to lifelong slavery.[6]

Death is the enemy. It is the single ubiquitous sign of the existence of disobedience and disorder. The fact that all men die sets in stone the truth that all men are sinners. "So death came upon all men" is the *universal condition of the cosmos* for death is not limited to disobedient human beings. The effects of disobedience reach to the very earth itself. Death is the epitome of Satan's power. If the cosmos is to be reconciled, if the perfect creation is to be restored, then death must be defeated. This is more than a matter of forgiveness for simply forgiving men does not necessarily entail that death is no longer a consequence of living. I could live blamelessly after forgiveness and still die as a result of my prior disobedience. In fact, death is still the universal experience of *forgiven* human beings. What must occur in order for the groaning of the creation to cease is the removal of death, the victory over the quintessential mark of a broken creation, the utter defeat of the last bastion of Satan's dominion. And this victory, the final victory, is accomplished on the cross. "That through death he might destroy" points to the cross, not simply as the

---

[6] Hebrews 2:14-15 ESV

place of human redemption, but as the place of *cosmic* restoration. Yeshua dies in order that death might be rendered powerless. The death on the cross reverses the entry of death into creation.

This is the context of John's analysis in John 3:16. Moses uses the very image of what causes death among the people. It is true that the serpents come as a result of disobedience, but the immediate issue for the people is *death*, not the serpents *per se*. Why does God tell Moses to form a symbol of the serpent? Doesn't that seem rather strange? Why doesn't God use the symbol of a lamb (recalling the Passover) or a symbol of the tablets of stone (recalling the covenant)? Why a snake? Perhaps the answer is found in the imagery of the serpent from the Egyptian culture. Certainly one of the marks of the divinity of Pharaoh was the headdress that included the serpent. Pharaoh held life and death in his hand. His serpent symbol was a sign of this power. Now God uses this same symbol to demonstrate that He alone has the power of life and death. Just as the plagues are battles between YHWH and the gods of Egypt, here once more we see God doing battle with an Egyptian symbol of divinity. Could the children of Israel, only a few days removed from the presence of the great serpent of Pharaoh, fail to miss the connection? The very thing that is causing them to die becomes the vehicle that God uses to bring life. The *power* of death, symbolized in the serpent of Pharaoh, is destroyed. God takes the pagan symbol and turns it into a sign of His sovereignty. Is this symbolism of Pharaoh's power essentially any different than the Roman symbol of the cross? Doesn't the cross symbolize the power of life and death in the hands of Rome?

YHWH takes that very symbol of the power of an alien government opposed to the purposes of God, and uses it to bring about the restoration of God's power and Kingdom. When Yeshua submits Himself to death at the hands of a pagan authority, He overcomes the paradigm symbol of that authority by converting it into a sign of God's vindication, of God's absolute sovereignty over death *and life*. What men thought they controlled becomes the vehicle that God uses to vindicate His control. Yeshua is no less rabbinic than Paul or John. He simply draws an analogy between two events in order to make a point about the power of life and death. He tells Nicodemus that when Nicodemus sees the Son of Man lifted up by an alien power he is not to see the sovereignty of a pagan government but rather the sovereignty of YHWH over *all* creation. Nicodemus will witness the execution of death and the destruction of Satan's last element of control.

John's commentary reiterates this connection. According to John's theological reflection, Yeshua comes to restore the entire creation. "For God so loved the *kosmos*" does not speak of the unique need of human beings. That is subsumed under the umbrella of the fall of creation itself. Death is the sure sign of creation's calamity, and death must be overcome before true restoration can be accomplished. Even though John's commentary includes a statement about whoever believes in Yeshua, the focus of the verse is on *life, eternal* life, life that will not end because death has been defeated. There is no mention here of forgiveness or mercy or pardon. The focus is much bigger. Life itself, life as God intended, is to be restored. Consider the statement John makes in John 3:17.[7] What does John mean when he uses the Greek verb *sozo* (to save)? If John is thinking about the Hebrew equivalents, he would be thinking about *yasha* (to save, to keep, to help), *palat* (to guard one's way, to save oneself) and *malat* (to escape). From the LXX we can determine that *sozo* could be translated with any one of these three Hebrew expressions. But when we examine the nuances of these three Hebrew terms, our picture of salvation changes. In Hebrew thought, saving is connected with having room to move. To be saved is to be removed from the confines of a narrow trap and be led to a broad expanse. This is accomplished by a stronger party rescuing a weaker party. This action is often associated with legal or military help. The result is not *freedom* but rather *dependence*. The paradigm examples of this help are related to God's *people*; His divine preservation of Israel. Salvation in Hebrew thinking also includes that idea of escape from immediate mortal danger or punishment. Only God can ultimately guarantee rescue, escape and deliverance. By the way, there are considerable numbers of verses in the Tanakh that indicate God does *not* help sinners or rescue the wicked. They do not enjoy the covenant relationship needed to experience God's rescue.

---

[7] *For God did not send his Son into the world to condemn the world, but in order that the world might be **saved** through him.* John 3:17 ESV

Let's apply these insights to John's claim. The first thing to notice is that John is not speaking directly about the *human* predicament. Just as his previous commentary made clear, John directs our attention to the *cosmos*, not the *anthropos*. Yeshua did not come to condemn *the world* but rather to rescue, help, deliver *the world*. Yes, we are part of the *cosmos*, but whatever Yeshua did it isn't limited to our need. If sin is the problem, it is not simply a *human problem*.

The recognition that Yeshua's entrance into the world is a *cosmic* issue forces us to ask, "Why does John tell us that He did not come to *condemn* the entire cosmos?" We need to ask this question because it drives us to look at sin in an entirely different way. This takes us back to Noah. The world was condemned to a watery death. The Genesis account makes it quite clear that sin had polluted the *earth* and God brought punishment upon *all* creation. If this is what John has in mind, then it implies that, as a result of sin, God would have been justified in condemning the earth – but by sending His Son He demonstrates that He will not do what He could have done. He will not condemn. He will rescue. Just as in the days of Noah, *everything is connected*. Our sins affect *everything*. They are not limited to the moral realm or to human ethics. Sin destroys God's *cosmic* order. Yeshua comes to restore that order.

Millard Erickson comments on this verse: "The purpose of the coming was atonement, and the Father was involved in that work."[8] But I think we

---

[8] Millard Erickson, *Christian Theology* (1st Edition), p. 806.

must understand salvation in cosmic terms. Theologically, the Christian idea of atonement is often limited to repairing the breach between God and humanity. But what John says is much, much bigger. It's not just about you and me being forgiven. It's not about getting to heaven. It's not about removing our guilt. It's about *saving the world* and everything about it. With this bigger picture in mind, are you still willing to say that Yeshua died on the cross to save you from your sins? Or are you simply the beneficiary of something that had a much bigger purpose? Perhaps we need to stop thinking of God's actions and Yeshua's purpose in such egotistical terms.

John adds another piece to our inquiry when he recounts Yeshua's remark, "And I, if I be lifted up from the earth, will draw all men to Myself."[9] Proper exegesis of this statement requires that we understand its context. Back up one verse and see how the opening statement fits this conclusion. "Now judgment is upon this world; now the ruler of this world shall be cast out."[10] Who is Yeshua talking about? The Devil?

We need to recognize that the Tanakh has almost nothing to say about "the Devil." Its sparing use of *ha-satan* indicates that this person (if we can even use this word) is best described as "the adversary" or "the accuser," and his role is carefully circumscribed and assigned *by YHWH*. He is not a free-wheeling, super powerful bad guy, wreaking havoc on everyone and everything. Basically, he does what God assigned him to do.

---

[9] John 12:32 NASB
[10] John 12:31 NASB

By the time we get to Yeshua's first-century view, more has been added to the role of *ha-satan*, but it is still a far cry from the typical Christian view of Satan. In fact, most of our ideas about Satan come from the Dark Ages. It takes a Christian paradigm shift to interpret Genesis 3 as an incarnation of Satan, to see Lucifer in Isaiah as Satan, and to identify the dragon in Revelation as Satan. We should probably note that Christian imagery of Satan typically associates him with the body of a pig or a goat. Where did those images come from? Can you guess?

If we follow the usual Christian orientation, Yeshua's statement about the "ruler of this world" becomes a circumlocution of Satan. But is this necessary? Put yourself in the place of the audience when Yeshua spoke these words. Whom would you think of as the *melech* (ruler, king)? Would you think of *ha-satan*, the obscure functionary of YHWH, or would you think of Caesar, the Emperor of the whole known world? What would the words mean to the *first* audience that heard them – the Jews of the first century? Would they conjure up images of red tails, pitchforks, half-goat, half-man Philistine or Canaanite male gods? Would they think like Dante?

If the statement about the "ruler of this world" is a description of Caesar, then the verse about being lifted up changes as well. There is little doubt that Yeshua is referring to the crucifixion but we must remember that crucifixion is a *Roman* symbol. It is, in fact, the paradigm Roman symbol of power over the Jews. If Yeshua is speaking to an audience that associates power with *Rome*, then His statement that the ruler of this world will lose all his power when the paradigm symbol of that power becomes a reality in the life of Yeshua, changes quite a bit about what we think. The power of the Roman cross is the power over life and death. Yeshua's crucifixion brought that power to an end. The Emperor's claim is finished. The kingdom of Rome has ended. It has been replaced by a Kingdom that will never end because its King will never die.

Why will all men be drawn to the one who is lifted up? Because without this King, without this victory, *death* still holds the power. All men will come because no man wants to die.

We need to carefully note that what Yeshua says seems to contradict an earlier statement. That is His statement that no one comes to Yeshua unless the Father draws him. But now He says that *He* will draw all men. How can both be true? The first statement about the Father is a statement about the role that YHWH plays in attracting men to the Son. The second statement is about the role that the victory over death plays in the hearts of men. One pushes. The other pulls.

Finally, notice the hypothetical condition of this statement. "*If* I be lifted up." Apparently the event is not *inevitable* (but notice that the ESV changes the translation to "when" making it a foregone conclusion). If it happens, its impact changes the world. But even Yeshua sees that it is possible that it will not happen. It must be a choice. Men are drawn to the victory over death, *all* men, by the way, not just Jews, because death is the universal problem. Sin as a universal problem only makes sense *within a community that recognizes sin*. But death affects everyone regardless of theology.

"*If* I am lifted up," then I will draw (the Greek is *helkyso*). The verb is future, active, indicative. The action will occur sometime in the future and will affect everyone. It has the sense of "dragging." Whether you and I want to or not, the very idea of a man who comes back from the dead is something we cannot ignore. We have to know what is beyond the grave. Every religion speaks about this. Only one offers proof. The crucifixion and the empty tomb are about power – power that only Yeshua can wield. Atonement might be accomplished by even fine flour (see Leviticus 14:21), but victory over death resides with no one else.

By the way, if the crucifixion destroys the power of death and death is the final stronghold of the enemy, then why do we credit the accuser with so much power and control? Who is he anyway?

There is one other clue that must be considered. The verb *sym* is found in the phrase "and *set* it on a pole." That verb tells us something else about the relationship between Moses' action and Yeshua's crucifixion. In 2 Kings 21:4 we see that the verb *sym* is used to describe the placement of the divine name. It is also used in 2 Samuel 17:25 and 1 Chronicles 11:25 to describe putting someone in a position of authority. In Genesis 21:18 we find the verb used to establish a new relationship. Finally (although there are other uses as well), we see the verb in Exodus 9:5 as a description of God's appointed times. The *Theological Wordbook of the Old Testament* notes that this verb is often connected with YHWH.[11] He "sets" the boundaries

---

[11] "The most frequent [of the idiomatic expressions using *rum*] is the use of God's being high to represent God's rank (II Sam.

of creation. He "makes" the descendants of Abraham as the dust of the earth. He "makes" the seed of David endure. He "appoints" the Torah as the law of Israel. He "brings about" miracles and afflictions. And He will "make" Israel His instrument of righteousness (Isaiah 41:15). It seems quite unlikely that Yeshua would not have known the connections with *sym* in His hint toward Numbers 21:9.

We are suggesting that there is a midrash *and* a remez in Yeshua's claim. The midrash ties *rum* (lifted up) to the event in the wilderness and points us toward exultation. The remez ties *sym* to the cross and points us toward God's sovereignty. Both of these connections demonstrate the *authority, power and divinity* implicit in the two terms. Neither points toward forgiveness.

Let's consider the connection to Number 21:9 once more.

*So Moses made a bronze serpent and set it on a **pole***. *And if a serpent bit anyone, he would look at the bronze serpent and live.* Numbers 21:9 ESV

The remez Yeshua employs when He points Nicodemus to this verse (John 3) also connects us to the Hebrew word *nes*, the word translated "pole" in this verse. Athol Dickson comments: "In other Scriptures, '*nes*' is translated as 'example' or 'banner.' In Isaiah 33:23, the word is translated as

---

22:47; Ps. 18:46; cf. Ps. 113:4; Is.6:1). Superiority of wisdom over a fool is thus described (Prov. 24:7). Deliverance is equated with height of the delivered one's head . . ." TWOT, *rum*, pp. 837-839 'sail,' and another word entirely is used for the pole or mast upon which the sail hangs. In fact, I can find no other place in the Hebrew scripture where anything else was mounted on a '*nes*.' Except for the bronze snake, it is always the other way around. The '*nes*' is never the pole; it is always the object lifted up on the pole. But here at the story of the serpents in the wilderness, the bronze serpent is mounted *on* the 'banner' or 'example'—the '*nes*.' In other words, here in this enigmatic little story I find a **symbol** (the bronze serpent) hung upon an **example** (the pole, *nes*) …Could it be that this word has been deliberately chosen to hint that it was not the serpent Israel must look to for deliverance, but the One **behind** the serpent?"[12]

Consider the implications involved in Yeshua's remez. Certainly Yeshua is aware that *nes* in every other instance means insignia or example. Therefore, the clue that he provides to Nicodemus suggests that Nicodemus will recognize the justification of Yeshua's claim when he sees the Son of Man as the insignia or example of the Father's handiwork. The Father will lift up the Son as a declaration of power and authority, just as Moses lifted up the serpent as an example of YHWH's power and authority. When will Nicodemus see this justification take place? When the Son dies on the cross. The pagan symbol of death will be overcome by the transposition wielded by God Himself. If Nicodemus has any doubt about Yeshua's claims, he need only wait until the end

---

[12] Athol Dickson, *The Gospel According to Moses: What I learned about Jesus from my Jewish friends*, p. 75.

32

and he will see how power and authority have been given to the Son. The proof is in the death.

We may add to this a comment by Marvin Wilson.

> It is not surprising that Isaiah, the Christological prophet *par excellence*, personifies *nes*. He says, "in that day the root of Jesse shall stand as an ensign to the peoples; him shall the nations seek" (11:10; cf. 11:12). So Israel's messianic king will be lifted up (cf. Jn 3:14; Phil 2:9) that all men might rally around him.[13]

Wilson observes that raising Yeshua as *nes* is about king and kingdom, just as Yeshua notes in his conversation with Pilate. The serpent on the pole points to the *sign of God's victory* over all pagan claims to power. Forgiveness? Yes, it's there too, but not on the cross.

Further examination of the use of *nes* leads us to Exodus 17:15 and additional clues about Yeshua's remark to Nicodemus.

Moses built an alter and named it The LORD is My banner. Exodus 17:15 NASB

Moses called it "YHWH *nissi.*" Actually, he names this altar with a compound divine name. "The

---

[13] Wilson, M. R. (1999). 1379 נסס In R. L. Harris, G. L. Archer, Jr. & B. K. Waltke (Eds.), *Theological Wordbook of the Old Testament* (R. L. Harris, G. L. Archer, Jr. & B. K. Waltke, Ed.) (electronic ed.) (583). Chicago: Moody Press.

LORD is my banner" is not a declarative statement applied to the altar. It is *God's name* memorialized by the altar.

Why should we care about this obscure reference to a name of God? The reason we care is because this obscure connection draws together Yeshua's remark to Nicodemus (John 3:14), Isaiah's declaration of the sign of the Messiah from the root of Jesse (Isaiah 11:10) and the pole of the serpent (Numbers 21:9). How does it do this? This verse reveals that the ensign (the *nes*), translated as "pole" in Numbers 21:9, is connected to God's name as the king of Israel. Nahum Sarna adds an important element: "The practice of giving names to altars is attested in Genesis 33:20, 35:7, and Judges 6:24. In none of these examples is any sacrifice mentioned. In fact, Joshua 22:26-27 explicitly excludes sacrificial rites from such a commemorative altar. The practice of designating commemorative altars seems to have ceased with the founding of the monarchy."[14]

Add this to the background of Yeshua's statement to Nicodemus. It seems to imply the following:

1. The imagery of the serpent on the pole is also an image of God's very name lifted up.
2. The imagery of the serpent on the pole carries suggestions of *kingdom*, power and military victory.
3. The serpent seems connected to Egyptian royalty. The pole (*nes*) seems connected to God Himself.

---

[14] Nahum Sarna, *Exodus, The JPS Torah Commentary*, p. 96.

4.   There is *no* connection to sacrifice or forgiveness.

5. If Yeshua intends Nicodemus to see the cross as an altar named for God, then the cross is associated with kings and kingdom (as is clear from the discussion with Pilate), not forgiveness.

6. The actual ensign on the cross is once again a *name* of the implement of torture, but it is the name "King of the Jews."

Is Yeshua's name memorialized on the cross? Certainly. Is His name truly 'King of the Jews'? Yes, it is. Is the cross a sign of power, a vehicle of transferred authority?   Yes.   Does this fit the exegesis of statements in the Tanakh about the "pole"? Yes. Is there any hint of sacrifice? No. Does that diminish in any way the cosmic impact of the event of the cross? Not at all. It only means that Christian interpretation of the event must be re-evaluated in terms of the Tanakh on which it is built.

Let's add these insights to the passage that Yeshua references.

*And YHWH said to Mosheh, "Make a fiery serpent, and set it on a **pole**. And it shall be that everyone who is bitten, when he looks at it, shall live." So Mosheh made a bronze serpent, and put it on a **pole**. And it came to be, if a serpent had bitten anyone, when he looked at the bronze serpent, he lived.* Numbers 21:8-9 ISR

Henru Pieters notes:

> What does John 3:14 and Exodus 17:15 have to do with Numbers 21:9? Can you

see the connection between the words pole, banner and cross? Because of strange translations, these words seem to be far removed from one another, but in Hebrew they all originate from one word. The Hebrew *nes* (pronounced as *nace*) is translated as *pole* in Numbers 21:8-9, and the first occurrence is in Exodus 17:15 as *Nissi* which means *my banner*, and is then used by Mosheh as a characteristic of YHWH. Mosheh only attributes this characteristic to YHWH after the victory by Yehoshua over Amalek, the victory of **life** over **death**.

Hebrew words can be traced back to a parent word that normally is a verb depicting everyday action in the Hebrew culture. The word *nes* comes from the verb *nasas* that means *to gleam from afar, to see a sign from far off*. Every tribe of Israel had their own banner with a symbol wherewith they would identify themselves. If you were travelling through the ancient land of Israel you would be able to see the banner of a certain tribe hanging at the entrance of one of their cities.

The verb *nasas* is related to the verb *nasa'* which means *to lift up* and is used in a wide variety of ways. The verb *nasas* only appears in the TaNaKh ("Old Testament") twice: in Zechariah 9:16 and Isaiah 10:18.

Making the connection between Numbers 21:9 and John 3:14 becomes clear when you realize that the *pole* or *banner* that Mosheh lifted up in the wilderness was a sign of **life** and **salvation** for the dying. The sign of the crucifixion means nothing to those who have not realized that they are dying and in need of life. All the people who looked upon the snake that Mosheh lifted up were those who sinned and had been bitten by the fiery serpents. If all people have sinned according to Romans 3:23, then all are in need of life and all need to look upon the death of the Messiah.

Tehillim (Psalms) 60:4 says, "You have given a banner (**nes**) to those who fear You, That it might be lifted up (**lehitnoses**) because of the truth. Selah."

[This is] a beautiful play on words in this Psalm that you can only see in Hebrew. Banner is **nes** and the words "might be lifted up" is **lehitnoses** and they are placed right next to each other reading like **nes lehitnoses**.[15]

If we follow the clues provided in the text, we do *not* arrive at the conclusion that the cross is the place of forgiveness of sin. Of course, we still have to deal with the way Paul understands the cross, but

---

[15] Henru Pieters, http://skipmoen.com/2013/03/28/puzzling-pole/

it seems clear from Yeshua's comment to Nicodemus that the cross is a sign of power, authority and appointment. That begs the question, "Power and authority over what?" And this leads us to the startling conclusion that the cross is God's sign of power and authority *over death*. We might put it like this: Sin was forgiven when the Lamb was slain *before* the foundation of the world (as we shall see). The sin sacrifice occurred in the heavenly Temple at the heavenly altar by a priest of the order of Melchizedek. Forgiveness was accomplished for Abraham and Paul in exactly the same way. But the broken world still experienced the result of sin – death – in spite of the forgiveness and grace of God. Death defiles the holy space of God's presence in His creation. Therefore, death also had to be defeated. The world had to know that death had been overthrown. And the cross, the instrument of death, became the vehicle for the demonstration that death no longer reigned supreme in the world. The guilt of sin was removed long before, but the world waited for the *sign* of the end of the curse that comes with disobedience. That sign is the cross. Death is the *sine qua non* of sin. All die because all have sinned. All are victims of death. But not after the cross! After the cross, sin no longer holds *all* captive. Death could not hold Him and neither will it hold all who follow Him. The ultimate and final threat of the power of sin has been destroyed.

And that's why Yeshua points to the snake.

Given our investigation so far, we should notice the inadequacy of the typical Christian answer to the question "Why Must the Son of Man 'Be Lifted Up'?"

"We have all sinned. Satan, often referred to as a serpent, has bitten every one of us and has infected us with a deadly poison – sin. We, in ourselves, have no antidote. The consequence of sin is death.

Jesus is the remedy. Just as God provided Israel a healing remedy, God has provided us with a remedy for sin's poison: he has given us his Son. Forgiveness of our sins is realised through Jesus who 'must be lifted up', a reference to the sacrificial death on the cross of our Lord Jesus Christ. Every sin we have committed is fully pardoned through the atoning death of Christ on the cross. He alone has the power to save us.

We look to Jesus. The Israelites looked to the bronze serpent God instructed Moses to make, and they were healed. We must look to Jesus for our spiritual healing. We cannot heal ourselves. Our response is one of trust, belief and faith in what he did on our behalf. We must trust the divine remedy if we are to be made right with God.

It is not what we do that saves us, but what Jesus has done for us. Through faith we accept from Jesus the forgiveness of sin through his death. In our baptism we are being identified with him through faith in his death, burial and resurrection. 'Having been buried with him in baptism and raised with him through ... faith in the power of God, who has raised him from the dead.' (Colossians 2:12)"[16]

Do you think Nicodemus, in his wildest dreams, could have supplied such an answer?

Nicodemus was a teacher of Israel. As such he would have been familiar with the Tanakh and the LXX. When we look at Number 21:9 in both the Tanakh and the LXX translation, we find words that imply exultation, not remedies for sin. Of course, that doesn't mean that the event of the bronze (copper) serpent in the wilderness cannot also be a midrash about forgiveness in Yeshua. But the point is this: the imagery itself and the language used do not *necessarily* point us in this direction. This would be quite well known to any Hebrew speaker. When Yeshua makes the midrash connection between *rum* and the event of the serpent in the wilderness, He points Nicodemus toward this conclusion – and we must follow His direction.

One of the cognates of *rum* is the word *teruma*. It means "contribution, offering, (and specifically) heave offering." Its specific cultic application is to the offering designated for the officiating priest (Leviticus 10:14-15). By the time of Yeshua, this word probably meant the general classification of

---

[16] http://www.bibleanswers.ie/short-bible-studies/64-jesus-christ/156-why-must-the-son-of-man-qbe-lifted-upq

"gift" offering. But in antiquity, it was never associated with anything other than a meat offering. That means it was always connected with a blood sacrifice and always related to the part of the sacrifice that only the designated priest could consume.

If we add this cognate to the basket of meanings that Yeshua alludes to in His use of the term, we find that His reference to being lifted up not only includes exultation, and in particular, exultation of the Most High God, but also a connection to the special designation for the priest and the priest's family in an offering that requires *specific* ritual adherence (see Leviticus 10). If we read the words in Leviticus, we find that this word, *teruma*, is an integral part of the sin offering. Perhaps Yeshua, who was an expert in Torah, deliberately used a word with connections not only to divine exultation but also to the necessity of perfect compliance to YHWH's instructions for the sin offering. Perhaps He is telling Nicodemus that He is *both*!

Ah, it's so deliciously complex. It's so deep and rich and stimulating, and it's so powerful. The one lifted up is exalted. He is also the one slain and offered, and because of Him, we can partake. These concepts are all wrapped up in the events in the wilderness and in a single word. Maybe that's why we need to read *one word at a time*!

Now we must consider the implications of this discovery for other exegetical problems.

Rooftop Problems

The assertion that "Jesus died on the cross for the forgiveness of sins" runs into another textual problem, this time from the actions of Yeshua Himself *prior* to His crucifixion. In Matthew 9:2ff. (and Mark 2:4ff.), Yeshua encounters a crippled man lowered through the roof. Yeshua proclaims that this man's sins are forgiven. When others present challenge His authority to forgive sins, He demonstrates His sovereignty by healing the man. This miracle story is well known and often used as a proof that Yeshua is divine (the opposing parties claim that only God can forgive sin). But in spite of the fact that this event demonstrates His divinity, it also raises a problem for the claim that forgiveness is established on the cross. Obviously, Yeshua proclaimed the man's sins forgiven *before* the crucifixion. We can hardly pretend that this announcement is only proleptic – that the crippled, but now healed, man actually had to wait until after the crucifixion before Yeshua's proclamation took effect. The man is *healed* as proof that his sins have been forgiven then. He doesn't have to wait until the cross. In what sense, then, can we say that forgiveness is made effective on the cross?

Rodney Baker provides some insight into this story.

> Now the Greek, the Aramaic and the Delitzsch Hebrew gospels all have the phrase "Take heart" as an imperative. Another English version says, "Be comforted, my son" (although the Greek apparently omits the possessive pronoun and says simply, "son").

Howard's Hebrew text, however, says something quite different. The phrase translated from Greek as "take heart" is not imperative – it is reflexive; the word *titchazzek* literally means, "You have strengthened yourself."

The word usually translated "forgiven" is also unusual. It is not the expected root *samech-lamed-chet* but instead the word is *n'muchlu*. The root is *nun-mem-lamed* which means "to tear away, to pluck."

The third thing is the phrase "*b'emunah ha'el*" – by the faithfulness of God. The full transliteration of what Howard's Hebrew text says is this:

v'yira yeshua emuntem vayomer l'cholah(?), titchazzek b'niy b'emunat ha'el n'muchlu avonotcha

Literally translated (only reversing a couple of words to make it readable in English):

"And Yeshua saw their faith and he said, 'You have strengthened yourself, my son; by the faithfulness of God, your iniquities are taken from you.'"[17]

Baker points out that this Hebrew variation would be perfectly acceptable to the religious teachers in the audience. God's faithfulness accounts for the man's forgiveness. But this variation doesn't explain the outrage of these same religious leaders. If all Yeshua proclaimed was the fact that God forgives, there would have been no argument. The

---

[17] Rodney Baker, "Take Heart,"
http://skipmoen.com/2013/01/05/

43

argument presupposes that Yeshua forgives, implying a claim to be equal with God. Furthermore, even if Howard's variant text is correct, the once-lame man has not followed any of the required protocols for receiving forgiveness. We can't find a way around the obvious claim of this story. Yeshua *forgives*, taking on the role of God. And if this is true, then the means of forgiveness granted to the lame man cannot depend on some action *yet to occur* at Calvary.

Of course, the rooftop problem isn't the only time that Yeshua grants forgiveness prior to the crucifixion. In fact, we might legitimately assume that every incident of healing involved forgiveness. This is the claim that James seems to make in his statement, "and the prayer offered in faith will restore the one who is sick, and the Lord will raise him up, and if he has committed sins, they will be forgiven him."[18] Although textual critics doubt the inclusion of John 7:53 to 8:11 in the original text, there is little doubt that the story of the woman caught in adultery typifies Yeshua's compassion and demonstration of forgiveness. But once again, this is forgiveness *prior* to the crucifixion. We might recall Yeshua's statement to the Pharisee, "For this reason I say to you, her sins, which are many, have been forgiven, for she loved much; but he who is forgiven little, loves little."[19] Once we recognize that the rooftop lesson is repeated again and again in Yeshua's practice, it is difficult, if not impossible, to maintain that forgiveness was not available prior to the crucifixion.

---

[18] James 5:15 NASB
[19] Luke 7:47 NASB

Jesus – the Only Sacrifice?

*"I am the way, the truth and the life; no one comes to the Father, **but** through Me."* John 14:6 NASB

It is common evangelical theology to assert that this statement from Yeshua excludes anyone who does not openly confess "Jesus" as savior and lord. Many preachers will confidently say that unless you accept "Jesus," you are going to hell. They conclude, therefore, that even those supposedly upright, ethical individuals who actually demonstrate compassion and trustworthiness are nevertheless deluded. They haven't met the requirement of "accepting Jesus." They are doomed.

There are two problems with this exegesis. The first is that *none* of the faithful Jews prior to the resurrection confessed Yeshua as their savior. What are we to do with Abraham, Noah, Phinehas, David, Isaiah, Hosea, Deborah and the list of others from the Tanakh? The standard answer is, "They lived before the Messiah came. They worshipped and served God as best they knew, but now things are different. Now that Jesus has lived and died, everyone must accept Him. Those Old Testament saints accepted Him *in principle* because they looked forward to His coming. But now we must accept Him as He has been revealed." There is some merit to this proleptic solution. But it opens a very wide door that is difficult to shut. If Abraham is saved because he looked forward to a Messiah whom he did not yet recognize, how is his favor with God any different than the grace God might show on the millions who live today *without really understanding that the Messiah is Yeshua?* You might include millions of God-fearing Jews, but I have more than that in mind. What about the Muslim who truly desires to serve God and who embraces *all* that he knows about God, but *all* that he knows is what Islam teaches. As far as he is concerned, Messiah Jesus is a Christian mistake. All he knows of Jesus is the animosity Christians have displayed toward Islam, beginning with the Crusades. Does this man really know *Yeshua*? Hardly! He knows a caricature of the real Yeshua; a caricature that he rightfully rejects. Exactly the same argument could be made for Torah observant Jews. What do they know of the real Yeshua? They only know the "Jesus" that the Church has portrayed, a Messiah that they must reject because that Christian Messiah stands in opposition to everything they know about God. If Abraham can be saved on the basis of *his knowledge of God*, then how is that different today? If you close the door on all God-fearers simply because they were born after 30 AD, what does that say about God's grace? Does God send a man to hell simply because he has *never* heard the truth?

Even if some theological contortions resolve this problem, another difficulty in Scripture remains. It is found in Revelation 13:8. The NIV translates, *"the Lamb that was slain from the creation of the world."*[20] 1 Peter 1:18-20 supports the idea that Yeshua's sacrifice occurred before the world was

---

[20] We will examine *why* the NASB and the ESV change the order of the prepositional phrases in this text so that the verse doesn't portray Yeshua's sacrifice preceding the creation. See below.

46

created, but wasn't revealed until some recognizable event in human history. In other words, the atonement for sin accomplished by the Son preceded (in some sense) the creation of the first human being. What happened in 30 AD may be connected in some way to this prior atonement, but the crucifixion is *not* the atoning event that took place *before the foundation of the world.*

If this is true, then Abraham, Noah, David and all the rest were "saved" because of this pre-creation sacrifice. Their standing before God relied on exactly the same foundation that supported Paul and Peter and John – and you and me. Abraham is *not* an exception to the rule. His salvation depended on Yeshua's sacrifice *before the foundation of the world* just as yours and mine. He just didn't know it!

Therefore, when Yeshua says "No one comes to the Father but through Me," He is stating an eternal truth, not an evangelical criterion. The eternal truth is that without His pre-creation sacrifice, *no one,* not even Abraham, comes to the Father. But this is not a requirement of confession. It is an ontological reality.

There are many people alive today, as there have been since Man first walked the earth, who know nothing of the true Messiah, either through ignorance or through deception. Nevertheless, they have hearts for God. They are Abraham, and just like Abraham, they come to the Father through the Son even if they don't recognize that fact. It is the task of those who do know Yeshua to present Him in His historical reality, but that doesn't alter the truth that He has been the needed sacrifice since before the world was created. The evangelical claim that you must confess this person or miss the blessing is myopic and misleading. Yes, if you know who He is, then you must do something about Him. But if you don't know, He is still your access to the Father. He is just hidden behind the words, "In the beginning."

Chapter Two

Examining the Texts

Before the Foundation

The implications of the verses we have been investigating create significant difficulties for the theological mantra that forgiveness occurs on the cross. After all, if there is no difference betwee4n the means of salvation for the Jews of the Old Testament and the believers in the New Testament, then the division between law and grace collapses. That division is revealed as an arbitrary theological schism, not a Scriptural distinction. And that calls into question the entire platform of supersessionism (replacement theology). If Abraham is saved by precisely the same heavenly Temple sacrifice that saves you and me, then the idea that the Church replaced Israel in order to usher in a new age of grace is false. Since an exegesis like this calls into question centuries of Christian doctrine, something had to be done; and the simplest way to fix this problem was to manipulate the offensive texts. That's exactly what happens in many of the translations of John's statement concerning the *timing* of the atoning sacrifice. The NASB translation is typical:

*and all who dwell on earth will worship him, every one whose name has not been written **from the foundation of the world** in the book of life of the Lamb who has been slain.* Revelation 13:8 (bold added)

What should we do with this prepositional phrase – "from the foundation of the world"? That's the big question. The NIV and the KJV put the phrase *at the end* of the sentence where it is in the original Greek text. Therefore, "from the foundation of the world" modifies the "Lamb slain;" but the ESV and the NASB *move* the prepositional phrase so that it modifies "name written." By moving this phrase, these translations rewrite history. They obscure the teaching that Yeshua was slain as the sacrifice *before the world was created*. According to these translations, the real issue is *when your name was written in the book*, not when Yeshua died as the sacrifice for sin.

There is *no* textual justification for this change. The Greek text clearly places the prepositional phrase *at the end* of the sentence. The only argument for moving it might be that the noun "name" is nominative (the subject) while the rest of the nouns (lamb, foundation, world) are genitives (showing possession) or that the prepositional phrase might be attached to the first verb (written) rather than the last verb (slain). Sometimes Greek sentences do displace prepositional phrases. But given the parallel teaching in 1 Peter 1:20 ("For he was foreknown[21] before the foundation of the world"), the decision to move the phrase appears

---

[21] The NASB translation of *proginosko* as "foreknown" possibly reflects a theological commitment to election. The parallel Hebrew word, found in the LXX in Judges 9:6 and 11:19 can also mean prophetically revealed knowledge. The question of the correct translation must be settled on the basis of an understanding of time in the Greek and Hebrew worldviews. See my book, *God, Time and the Limits of Omniscience*.

theologically motivated, not textually motivated. Leon Morris, a world-renowned Greek scholar, comments: *"From the foundation of the world* should be taken with *slain* (cf. 1 Pet. i. 19f.) rather than with *written* (though some prefer to take it this way and understand it of election as Eph. 1. 4)."[22] Even Morris notes that the decision to move the phrase is based in a prior commitment to the doctrine of election, not to the straightforward reading of the text.

What does this mean? If we accept the NIV and KJV translations, we are presented with a statement that Yeshua's sacrifice occurred before the world was created. From a Western perspective, this seems impossible. After all, history is *linear*. Something cannot have occurred *before* it takes place. Yeshua died in 30 AD, not before the creation. But this is a Western view of time. In Hebraic thought, history is seen in repeating cycles. The cycles are not *exactly* the same (as we find in Buddhism). They are patterns that play out like a point on a turning wheel, as it travels down the road. History moves forward (to use a spatial analogy) but it is cycloidal at the same time. Furthermore, the *reality* of eternity is what happens in heaven, not on earth. Just as there is a heavenly Tabernacle and a heavenly altar, there are also heavenly sacrifices. The earthly representations of these heavenly realities are shadows of the truth, understood in part now, but somehow hidden in their full meaning until heaven and earth are renewed.

---

[22] Leon Morris, *The Revelation of St. John*, Tyndale New Testament Commentaries, pp. 160-170.

When the translators of the ESV and the NASB moved the phrase, they erased the Hebraic view of cyclical patterns and the Hebraic view of this shadow world. They rewrote eternal, heavenly history to match our earthly sequence of events. Without informing the reader, they simply altered the Hebraic perspective of Yohanan (John) and made his words reflect Greek thinking about time. They also shifted the salvation argument by eliminating the possibility that Yeshua's heavenly sacrifice preceded *all* human access to the Father. In other words, this textual rearrangement removes the possibility that Yeshua has always been and will always be (since the foundation of the world) the *only* access to the Father *even if the recipient of grace doesn't know it.*

Subtle, isn't it? Subtle and extremely dangerous. The implications are staggering. By moving the prepositional phrase, they created a seismic shift in God's timeline. Now it is "before Christ/after Christ." But in Hebrew it is "always Christ."

Now that we see this New Testament Greek text informs us that the sacrifice occurred before the foundation of the world, we must examine the meaning of the phrase "foundation of the world" in order to discover what is hidden behind it. However, our discovery should not be taken to mean that the readers in the first century were blind to these insights. After all, they were reading the original Greek text from a Hebraic point of view. What we are about to "discover," they already knew.

There are two Greek words translated "foundation" in English texts. The first is *katabole*. We find crucial occurrences of this word "foundation" is the following texts:

> Matthew 13:35
> Matthew 25:34
> John 17:24
> Ephesians 1:4
> Hebrews 4:3
> Hebrew 9:26
> 1 Peter 1:18-20
> Revelation 17:8

We will examine each of these texts to determine meaning in use, and discover relationships to the Tanakh.

The second Greek word translated "foundation" is *themelios*. The crucial occurrences of *themelios* are found in:

> 1 Corinthians 3:12
> Ephesians 2:20
> 1 Timothy 6:19
> 2 Timothy 2:19
> Hebrew 6:1
> Hebrew 11:10
> 1 Peter 5:10
> Revelation 21:19

We must also examine these occurrences to determine if any additional insights can be added. However, it will not be sufficient to simply investigate the Greek words used in the New Testament; we must also examine their Hebrew equivalents. We must do this for two reasons. First, whatever Yeshua said about the relationship between the cross, atonement and God's eternal plan was not spoken in Greek. It was spoken in Hebrew and *translated* into Greek. That means that the real meaning of His comments must be found in the Hebraic equivalents. Even if we examine the Greek letters of Paul and Peter and John, we know that their ideas originate in the Tanakh and with the teachings of Yeshua. So although they write in Greek, they are also attempting to capture Hebraic ideas.

Secondly, scholars recognize that New Testament Greek does not find its meanings in the classical Greek of Homer, Aristotle or Plato. It finds its meanings in the LXX, the Greek translation of the Hebrew Scriptures. The Greek New Testament is heavily influenced by the way Greek is used in this ancient translation, often completely altering the meaning of a classical Greek word to fit new contexts.[23] New Testament authors rely on these connections to bring their ideas to a Greek-reading population. Therefore, behind most important Greek words are Hebrew ideas, and we will have to

---

[23] There is no better example than the common Christian word *agape*, a word that is all but ignored in classical Greek but becomes the centerpiece of New Testament thought. Another prime example of the Hebraic underpinnings of New Testament Greek words is found in *eleeo* (to show mercy). The Hebrew word most often translated by *eleeo* is *hesed*, but it is quite clear that *eleeo* does not and *cannot* capture the multifaceted elements of *hesed*. Our English translations follow the LXX *eleeo* when dealing with *hesed*, diminishing the rich implications of the Hebrew word. For more on this issue, see my articles on *hesed* on my website (skipmoen.com).

explore these Hebrew ideas in order to understand why the New Testament authors picked these particular Greek words.

We will proceed in steps. First we will examine one key Greek word. Next we will investigate its Hebrew equivalents. Then we will take the next Greek word, proceeding in the same manner until we have covered the critical terms in both Greek and Hebrew. Next we will draw conclusions from our investigation and see if those conclusions would make sense to a first century Jewish audience. Finally, we will see if our justified conclusions align with popular Christian notions about the cross. Then we will have solved the cross-word puzzles.

katabole – Examining the Greek texts

katabole – foundation, beginning (Strong's #2602) TDNT III, 620-21

In English translation, *katabole* has several different expressions. "Laying down," is used of physical structures as well as (metaphorically) sexual male propagation ("sowing seed"). *Katabole* is used in the technical phrase "foundation of the world" to denote time or the eternal plan of God's salvation (cf. Matthew 25:34). With the proposition *pro*, it describes God's eternal love for His Son (John 17:24), the election of His people (Ephesians 1:4) and the election of His Son (1 Peter 1:20).

The rabbis use this term for the divine foreordination of human destiny from the beginning of creation (Pesikta de Rabbi Kahana 21, 145a; Midrash Esther 1, 1 (82a); Tanchuma 48a;

55

Tanchuma 26a.) The Hebrew equivalents are typically *kun* or *yasad*.

Let's examine each occurrence from our list to see what we can determine about the meaning of the term in use.

Matthew 13:35 *so that what was spoken through the prophet might be fulfilled, saying, "I will open my mouth in parables; I will utter things hidden since the foundation of the world."* NASB. Matthew 13:35 uses the term *katabole* as a translation of the Hebrew text of Psalm 78:2. But we immediately notice that this is odd since the text in the Tanakh does not use the normal Hebrew equivalent of *katabole*, i.e., either *kun* or *yasad*. The text of Psalm 78:2[24] uses *mini-qedem*, "from of old, from antiquity." This is not the same as "since the foundation," as the Hebrew equivalent clearly shows. Why did Matthew (in translation) shift the meaning so that it has direct implications of either *kun* or *yasad*? Specifically, why did Matthew incorporate the phrase "since the foundation" when this expression is not found at all in the passage in Psalms?

Here we are confronted with a first century Jewish rabbinic technique. Matthew typically *alters* citations from the Tanakh to fit his purposes. This does not mean that he considers the words of the Tanakh any less sacred or inviolable. It simply means that Matthew addressed passages from the Tanakh as if each one is a *remez*, a hint at

---

[24] "I will open my mouth in a parable, I will utter dark saying of old." Psalm 78:2 NASB in Hebrew, *eftecha vemashal pi abiah chidot mini-qedem*

something deeper. Matthew then moves from this *remez* to an application of the text to some event or saying in the story of Yeshua.[25] In this case, Matthew wants to establish a precedent for Yeshua's use of parables, a teaching style the deliberately hides elements of the spiritual insights. He uses the passage from Asaph's psalm because it was typically understood as the role of the recognized prophet. For Matthew, the similarity is the connection with the idea of parable, in Greek *parabole*, in Hebrew *mashal*. A prophet is one who reveals what is hidden (the "dark sayings of old"). Matthew likens the teaching style of Yeshua to that of the prophet in the Tanakh, in order to give credence and authority to the claims he will make about Yeshua. Matthew's use of this psalm is a demonstration that Yeshua "stands in the line of God's authorized spokesmen and his chosen method of teaching has good OT pedigree."[26]

As far as our analysis is concerned, we learn that even Greek translations incorporating the crucial word *katabole* do not necessarily express the same

---

[25] As an example, consider Matthew's use of Jeremiah's prophecy in Matthew 2:18 (citing Jeremiah 31:15). Matthew not only alters the syntax and grammar, he applies a prophecy that has nothing to do with the *death* of the subjects to an event that is all about the death of the subjects. Matthew ignores the context of Jeremiah's prophecy because he wants to establish a connection between Yeshua and prophetic fulfillment. The similarity of events is enough for Matthew to "see" in Jeremiah a connection to Yeshua. Much of Messianic prophecy follows this pattern, highlighting connections seen only in hindsight that were unrecognizable as prophetic at the time they were proclaimed.

[26] R. T. France, *The Gospel of Matthew*, The New International Commentary on the New Testament (Eerdmans, 2007), p. 530.

concept in Hebrew. The Greek text is not always a reliable source for direct comparison with Hebrew thought, and in English translation, this disparity is often exacerbated.

Matthew 25:34 *"Come, you who are blessed of My Father, inherit the kingdom prepared for you from the foundation of the world."* If you turn to the Beatitudes in Matthew 5, you will find that each one begins with the Greek word *makarioi*. This word should not be translated "blessed are" since it is not a verb and it does not carry with it the idea of some favor bestowed on another. As I have pointed out in my book, *The Lucky Life*, this word is about a state of bliss brought about by the actions of men. It is a *description* of the condition of a person, not a formula for receiving some spiritual blessing. But when we come to Yeshua's statement about the final judgment, we don't find the word *makarioi*. Instead, we find *eulogemenoi* (from the verb *eulogeo*). The change is important. The implications are entirely different than those found in the normal "blessed are" statements. The problem, of course, is that you don't even see a hint at the difference when you read the Bible in English. *Eulogeo* (literally, "to speak well of") is a stronger theological statement about the favor of God than the usual *makarios* that implies a condition brought about by the actions of men.[27] The favor these believers will inherit is related to the Kingdom.

Eulogeo is specifically associated with the act of showing favor toward someone else. In the first

---

[27] See my book, *The Lucky Life: The Backwards Beatitudes.*

century, this is typified by the action of a king toward one of his subjects. The king represents power. He has the authority to grant or remove privileges or rewards. In this verse, Yeshua uses this well-known fact about kings and kingdoms to describe the action taken by the absolute sovereign at the Final Judgment. Since *eulogeo* is the standard Greek translation of the Hebrew *barak*, it is often associated with God's favor. In this case, the grace and goodness of God is exhibited in the selection of the righteous to eternal reward. Because the word *eulogeo* is connected to the Hebrew *barak*, we recognize that Yeshua undoubtedly used *barak* when He spoke these words, and that means that He employed a verb that implies that God is the only source of true favor; i.e., that abundant life depends entirely on God's goodness and faithfulness.

This means that we must look to the Tanakh in order to understand what Yeshua meant, and when we look to the use of *barak* as an action of God in the Tanakh, we discover that context of the Tanakh is built on the idea that God is the only one who can grant life. The Tanakh clearly states that He is willing to give life to all who trust in Him. But that trust is demonstrated in faithful loyalty to Him. In other words, *barak* is commonly associated with *hesed* and *'emet*. Favor is *not* indiscriminate. While the invitation to enjoy God's favor knows no boundaries, the resulting reward requires reciprocal action. *Eulogeo* follows obedience.

Consider the implications of the connection between *eulogeo* and *barak* and the statement at the end of this verse. All of this was prepared "before the foundation of the world." This means that the relationship between invitation and reciprocal obedience has been in place *since the beginning*. It didn't change when Yeshua was born. It wasn't altered on the cross. It is exactly the same connection found in Abraham and in Paul. This un-Beatitude is eternal. And it will still be in place when the Final Judgment occurs.

The verse implies that this is not something that came into being after the ministry of Yeshua. God's eternal purposes are now fulfilled – purposes which have been part of His grand design since before the creation of the earth. It is important to note that the assumption behind this statement is the power and authority implied in the declaration of the king. The context makes this clear. Verses 31 to 33 speak of the time when the Son of Man "comes in His glory" and sits on the throne. This is the time when "all the nations will be gathered before Him" and He will execute judgment. The context shows us that this event has been part of the plan of God from the very beginning. Once again, we are confronted with a statement that even the final judgment is no afterthought. The use of *katabole* points us back to the very beginning of God's creative work regarding Man, not to a time initiated by the event on the cross.

Ephesians 1:4 *even as he chose us in him before the foundation of the world, that we should be holy and blameless before him, in love.* ESV

Here the phrase *pro kataboles kosmou* (before the foundation of the cosmos) is a temporal indicator that the election of the people of God in Christ was established prior to the creation. But notice that the prior verse suggests that this action occurred in the heavenlies. It is both spatially and temporally prior to creation. Paul states that "every spiritual blessing" found in the heavenlies is ours because it has been determined to be so before the foundation of the world. Does that not include the blessing of restored relationship with the Father, drawing close to Him because He has made provision to deal with our disobedience? When did this blessing of forgiveness occur? According to Paul in this passage, it was put in place "before the foundation of the world."

Christian theology that marks the point of restoration at the crucifixion must read Paul's remark as proleptic; that is, Paul is merely *anticipating* the final outcome, noting it was always the *intention* of God. But the verb here ("chose") is an aorist indicative indicating an action *already completed in the past*. It is hard to see how Paul's statement can mean anything but an action *finished* before the world began. This is why this verse is often cited as a proof-text for election and predestination. But this involves several complex theological issues, not least of which is how this choice can be determined *before* the required salvific event of the cross is accomplished. Suggesting that the cross was also predetermined plays havoc with any concept of the free will of the Son. If God determined the outcomes of all events prior to the creation, then how are we to make sense of the prayer in the Garden of Gethsemane?

John 17:24 *"... to see My glory that You have given Me because You loved me before the foundation of the world"* ESV

In the high priestly prayer, Yeshua states that the glory He has received is based on a love that pre-dates creation. It is important to note that the verb *didomi* (to give) is a perfect, active indicative. That means this action *has already been accomplished in the past,* but has continuing application in the future. We would have expected Yeshua to say, "The glory that You *will give* Me." After all, He has not yet been crucified. But He states that this glory is already His. In fact, He makes the same claim about the glory found in the disciples. He has given them (*dedokas* – perfect, active, indicative) the same glory that the Father has given Him. This suggests that the redemptive plan that results in the glorification of the Son was already in place prior to the incarnation, prior to the creation; and if this is true, redemption cannot depend on the space-time event on the cross. Redemption, as the basis of Yeshua's glorification, comes *prior* to any human involvement and depends on the purposes of the Father, not of the actions of the Romans. What happens on the cross is the manifestation, the sign, of something that took place in eternity past, an event that grows out of the love of the Father *before* the world began. Yeshua prays that His disciples with now *see* what has been true since before the beginning. But notice that Yeshua does not mention forgiveness or mercy or atonement. His focus is on *glory*, not some provision for dealing with the sins of men; and glory is the summary word for power and authority, for sovereignty, for recognition of absolute divinity. Once more *katabole* (foundation) is tied to *doxa* (glory), not to *aphesis* (forgiveness, pardon).

Certainly every Christian believer is familiar with the Greek word – *doxa*. In days past, it was incorporated into a ritual of Sunday worship. We sang the *doxology*; but did we ever really understand the idea of glory? Yes, we realized that God is glorious, that His splendor is manifest in all that He does, that His reflection is found in holiness, justice, mercy and compassion; but how is it possible that Yeshua could say this *doxa* has been given to us? Are we filled with splendor? Are we reflections of holiness? Do we manifest goodness, justice and mercy? It's just as difficult to see this in His followers. It's even more difficult when we notice that the verb here (*dedoka*) means that what Yeshua has given in the past has continuing result in the present (the perfect tense in Greek). The two verb tenses are the same. God gave glory to Yeshua (an action in the past with continuing results in the present). We understand that. Yeshua put aside divinity and became a man, but the Father glorified Him – gave Him back what He put aside – and He has that glory now and forever. But you and me? How did Yeshua give us *glory* and how does it still show up today?

Leon Morris provides this explanation: "Just as His [Yeshua's] true glory was to follow the path of lowly service culminating in the cross, so for them [the disciples] the true glory lay in the path of lowly service wherever it might lead them."[28]   Morris

---

[28] Leon Morris, *The Gospel According to John*, NICNT, p. 734.

amplifies this comment by adding that "the apostles are right with God and therefore they are supremely significant. They have the true glory. They are walking in the way of God."[29] That sounds so nice, but it doesn't seem to be true. Yeshua spoke these words just before His arrest. *None* of the apostles remained loyal to Him after that event. Is that "walking in the way of God"? Did they "take up the cross and follow"? It seems that Morris' comment is only accurate *after* the resurrection, but Yeshua says that He has already given them the equivalent glory of what He received. The perfect tense does not imply that they *will* receive it at some later point in time. It implies that the gift has already been given. Morris considers the "way of the cross" to be the "way of true glory." We might agree, but how can this be true of the apostles when Yeshua makes this statement? Maybe we just don't understand what "glory" means.

One thing is certain. Yeshua wasn't speaking Greek when He uttered these words. So examining the meaning of *doxa* is not going to help much. *Doxa* is used as the translation of twenty-five different Hebrew words in the LXX. But primarily it is associated with the Hebrew *kavod*. Rooted in the language of the land, *kavod* is about what is heavy, what has weight – and therefore has importance and significance. But since YHWH is invisible, *kavod* is used as a description of His *manifestation*. He *reveals* Himself as glorious. We find this sense of the word in the description of the *Shekhinah* falling on the Tabernacle, the vision of Ezekiel, the illumination of Moses' face and the

---

[29] *Ibid.*, p. 734-735.

transfiguration of Yeshua. *Kavod* is a description of the revelation of God in His acts in creation and salvation. Above all, it speaks of God's *honor*, exhibited in His self-revelation.

What does this mean to us for understanding Yeshua's statement? "The manifestation, self-revelation and honor you have given me, I have given to them." Has Yeshua passed to us the manifestation of YHWH? Have we become the vehicles of His honor? If we think of "glory" as a kind of possession, as a *state* of being that is somehow attached to us in the way that we acquire a gift when it becomes our property, then we will misinterpret Yeshua's declaration. We will think of "glory" from a Greek paradigm, as though receiving glory is an expression of a quality that is now ours. "Glory" becomes an adjective in much the same way that "saved" becomes an adjective.

But if we think in Hebrew, then we notice the *kavod* is not something we possess. It is an act that we participate in. We *become* the manifestation. We *become* the honor and the revelation. We don't *have it*. We *are* what it is as it is displayed *through us*. Glory is a description of Yeshua *as He fulfills the purposes of the Father* because in that process He manifests the truth of YHWH. It is the same for us. Yeshua gives us the means and the opportunity to become the process of God's self-revelation. We are glory, the glory of the Father, precisely as Yeshua was the glory of the Father, *when we manifest the Father* in our actions.[30]

---

[30] Abraham Heschel captures this idea when he speaks of the Jewish way of life. "We do not confess our belief in God; we adore Him. We do not proclaim our belief in revelation; we

Reading the text from a Hebraic point of view helps us see that this statement, and the other related statements in the priestly prayer of John 17, are not about a death on the cross for the forgiveness of sin. They are about the manifestation of YHWH's will, the visible sign of YHWH's purpose and power. What matters most in the event of the cross is that the world will see God's handiwork vindicating the ministry of His Son. What matters is the display of the Kingdom!

Hebrews 4:3 *"... although His works were finished from the foundation of the world"* ESV

In a discussion of the promise of entering into God's rest, the author cites Psalm 95:11, demonstrating that God's wrath will be poured out on the wicked who will *not* enter into rest in spite of the fact that God's works (plural) were finished (*ginomai* – to be born) from (*apo*) the foundation (*kataboles*) of the world. The critical adverb is *kaitoi* (although). The author suggests that even though God's sovereign hand has already birthed the course of the world, this does not mean that those who do not believe were determined from the beginning to experience God's wrath. It is their resistance to the truth that precipitates their fate. The accomplishment of God's works prior to the foundation of the world does not predestine them to

---

utter our gratitude for it. We do not formulate the election of Israel; we sing it. Thus our liturgy is no mere memorial to the past; it is an act of participating in Israel's bearing witness to the unity, uniqueness, love and judgment of God. It is an act of joy." *Man's Quest for God: Studies in Prayer and Symbolism* (Aurora Press, 1998), p. 78.

punishment. As we discover in Hebraic thought, the purposes of God, manifest in creation, are *progressive*, not static. The Hebrew perspective looks at the *whole* of the action from inception to completion as if it were one, unified movement. The works of God prior to creation are not uniquely different than the fulfillment of those works in creation. God always starts what He finishes.

Hebrews 9:26 *"Otherwise, He would have needed to suffer often since the foundation of the world;"* NASB

In this crucial passage concerning the sacrifice offered by Yeshua, the author explicitly states that Yeshua's sacrifice was not made in the tabernacle "made with hands," "but into heaven itself" (Hebrews 9:24). The author argues that it is *impossible* that the Messiah could have made the required sacrifice in the earthly temple because sacrifices made in the earthly temple "cannot make the worshipper perfect in conscience" (v. 9). Furthermore, the ritual sprinkling of blood in the earthly temple merely sanctifies the flesh, a necessary but insufficient condition of the worship of God. But Yeshua entered the heavenly temple as a high priest of a different order (since He was not a Levite as required by the Mosaic code), offering His blood on the heavenly altar *once* rather than repeatedly as the shadow ritual on earth required.

Rabbi Robert Gorelik argues compellingly that the author of Hebrews gives us a picture of the sacrifice of Yeshua in the heavenly temple. In other words, the forgiveness of sin does not occur on earth. Gorelik notes that nothing about the crucifixion meets the requirements of a sin offering. Instead, that offering is made in the heavenly temple where the shedding of Yeshua's blood is performed according to the heavenly requirements of the sin offering.

Gorelik points out that Yeshua could not have entered the earthly Holy of Holies in order to make such an offering because He was not a Levite. He was from the tribe of Judah, and therefore was prohibited to enter the Holy of Holies on earth. But the heavenly temple has a different priestly order, the order of Melchizedek, and the author of Hebrews takes pains to assure his readers that Yeshua is of that order. Yeshua enters the heavenly Holy of Holies and fulfills the requirements of the sin offering *once* and only *once*, unlike the priests of the order of Levi who must annually offer a sacrifice for the people – two temples, two priestly orders, two different consequences.

Perhaps this helps us understand why the shedding of blood of *one* man can have universal effect. On earth, one man may die for another. But how can one man die for all? No earthly mathematics can explain such an extension of grace. But in heaven things are different. The sacrifice of one is sufficient for the forgiveness of many, especially so when the One is God Himself.

This helps us understand the claim that Yeshua made this offering *before the foundation of the world*. Death on the cross didn't occur before the formation of the world. But it isn't the cross that is in view here. The sin offering sacrifice for Mankind takes place in heaven's timeframe, not earth's. Its result is *manifested* on earth at the time of the death and resurrection. What Yeshua accomplished in heaven finally becomes visible on earth, but that does *not* mean that forgiveness through the shedding of the blood of the Lamb was not available *before* the crucifixion. Forgiveness through the shedding of the blood of the Lamb was available as soon as the sacrifice was offered in the heavenly temple. In other words, Abraham was "saved" in exactly the same way that you and I are "saved." Earthly calendars make no difference. The point is that the cross event is a manifestation of the *results* of forgiveness. It is not the *action* of forgiveness. The cross finds its meaning in the *consequences* that the heavenly sacrifice has for the final removal of defilement on earth. The cross is the event in which God manifests His ultimate power over death, since death is the symbol of the result of sin.

This implies that the sacrificial system *here on earth* hasn't ended. It is merely on hold until the rebuilding of the Temple. But, of course, the Temple in heaven has never been destroyed. It remains throughout eternity as the place of God's sacrifice for Man's sin.

1 Peter 1: 20 *He was foreknown before the foundation of the world but was made manifest in the last times for the sake of you* ESV

Peter's claim is in concert with the claim of the author of Hebrews. The sacrifice of the "precious blood of Christ" is associated with knowledge in place before the foundation of the world. Here we have several crucial Greek terms that must be investigated. The first is *proginosko* – to have intelligence knowledge beforehand. *Proginosko* is constructed from the root verb *ginosko* and the preposition *pro*. "As distinct from *aisthánesthai, ginōskō* emphasizes understanding rather than sensory perception, and as distinct from *dokein* it is a perception of things as they are, not an opinion about them. Related to *epistémē, gnōsis* needs an objective genitive and suggests the act of knowing rather than knowledge as such."[31] If Peter employs the word as an accurate description of God's knowledge of the sin sacrifice of Yeshua before the foundation of the world, then this verb implies full comprehension of the event and its consequences. In other words, the impact of this sacrifice was already fully in view when God counted Abraham righteous. Abraham might have been unaware of the *prior* expiation of sin, but God was not. Furthermore, it is not necessary to take *proginosko* as if it has *predictive* influence over the event of Calvary. The fact that the sacrifice occurred in the heavenly Temple prior to the foundation of the world implies that God's full knowledge of the remedy for sin is only "foreknown" from our perspective. For God, it is an accomplished reality. The temporal position of the sacrifice was before the creation of Mankind, and is therefore *prior* to our awareness of it; but from God's point of view, the sacrifice had already been made when Mankind was created. Therefore, it was not foreknowledge to God.

---

[31] Kittel, G., Friedrich, G., & Bromiley, G. W. (1985). *Theological Dictionary of the New Testament* (119). Grand Rapids, MI: W.B. Eerdmans.

The Hebrew translation of *ginosko* is typically *yada'*. However, *yada'* has a much broader range of meaning than simply cognitive apprehension. It can include even physical experiences such as illness and sexual encounters, things not usually thought of as cognitive. "Knowledge of God, then, is acknowledgment of his grace, power, and demand, so that we have knowledge, not as mere information or mystical contemplation, but only in its exercise."[32] *Yada'* is knowing as a function of acting – not simply mental acquisition. Applied to Peter's statement, this means that God's knowing the sacrifice carries with it the execution of the sacrifice. Once more we have strong evidence that the sacrifice *actually took place* before the foundation of the world.

Peter states that we only recognized the importance of this prior event when it was *manifested* in our temporal framework. The Greek verb *phaneroo* indicates that the event of the sacrifice became clear to us, was revealed to us, at a time not synonymous with its actual occurrence, but rather after it had occurred. The manifestation is not the reality. It is only the evidence of the prior event. We might consider an analogy in human affairs. If I perform an experiment in the chemistry lab and the mixing of two substances results in a new precipitant, the reality of the reaction occurs prior to my observation of the precipitant, but I do not observe that reality until I notice the evidence it produces. The evidence reveals the truth about something that

---

[32] Kittel, G., Friedrich, G., & Bromiley, G. W. (1985). *Theological Dictionary of the New Testament* (120). Grand Rapids, MI: W.B. Eerdmans.

has already occurred, but the evidence is *not* the reaction itself. In like manner, we may say that the cross is the manifestation of a prior reality. It is the evidence that something has already happened. In this case, Peter tells us that the cross is the revelation that the sacrifice for sin took place before the foundation of the world. The cross is not the reality of forgiveness. It is merely the observable evidence of the prior event.

Revelation 13:8 *All inhabitants of the earth will worship the beast—all whose names have not been written in the Lamb's book of life, the Lamb who was slain from the creation of the world.* NIV

This critical verse containing a clear statement about the slaying of the Lamb before the foundation of the world has been altered in translation (ESV, NASB, RSV, NTL) to shift the prepositional phrase "from the foundation of the world" so that it modifies "names written in the Book" rather than "Lamb slain."[33] There appears to be no linguistic justification for this shift, with the possible exception of a similar phrase found in Revelation 17:8. We will deal with that shortly. The Greek phrase (*apo kataboles kosmou*) is equivalent to the phrase used in 1 Peter 1:20 (the only difference is the opening preposition *pro* rather than *apo*) and Peter's usage clearly concerns an event *prior* to creation. Why would the translators of the text shift the prepositional phrase? By moving the phrase to

---

[33] NASB is typical of this transformation. "All who dwell on the earth will worship him, *everyone* whose name has not been written from the foundation of the world in the book of life of the Lamb who has been slain."

modify "names in the Book," the verse implies that those who are saved are chosen (accounted for) *prior to creation*. This is a theological restatement of one of the central tenets of Calvinism – unconditional election. The doctrine asserts that God *foreknows* who will be saved and therefore grace is applied only to these chosen ones. God's omniscience entails His knowledge of the actual individuals who respond to His call. God knows their names prior to creation. But this is not *translation*. This is theology inserted into the text, and in this case, requiring that the order of the Greek text be altered to fit the doctrine. Furthermore, the doctrine itself rests on a Greek view of time, a view not shared by the Hebrew worldview and probably not shared by Peter.[34] There are significant and fatal problems associated with this idea of time. Here it is sufficient to note that the underlying assumptions about the relationship between temporal passage and omniscience are not as simple as the doctrine makes it seem. Inserting this idea into the text is unwarranted and misleading.

Now let's deal with the only other text where placement of the phrase "before the foundation of the world" might justify this shift in Revelation 13:8.

Revelation 17:8 *The beast that you saw was and is not, and is about to come up out of the abyss and to go to destruction. And those who dwell on the earth*

---

[34] For a full discussion of the difference between the Greek and Hebrew views of time and the impact on doctrinal development, see my book, *God, Time and the Limits of Omniscience*.

shall wonder, whose name has not been written in the book of life from the foundation of the world, when they see the beast, that he was and is not and will come. NASB

According to current English translations, the Greek phrase *apo kataboles kosmou* in this text modifies "name has not been written." Any linguistic justification for shifting the prepositional phrase in Revelation 13:8 (as we noted above) must be based on the position of the phrase in this verse. But this justification cuts both ways. If I am allowed to move the prepositional phrase in 13:8 to match what I find in 17:8, am I not also allowed to move the phrase in 17:8 to another part of the verse? Why can't I move the phrase to modify "dwellers on earth" rather than "name not written in the book"? Then 17:8 would read, "and the dwellers on earth from the foundation of the world whose name has not been written in the book of life . . ." If the prepositional phrase location is fluid in 13:8, why isn't it also fluid in 17:8? Rewriting 17:8 in this way seems no more or less linguistically possible than the emendation proposed by various translations of 13:8.

There is also some paradigmatic justification for emending Revelation 17:8. The verse concerns the visibility of the beast. It employs the phrase "was, and is not, and is to come," commonly understood by end-times theologians as an allusion to resurrection. Whatever the actual meaning of this expression, it is clear that the circumstances surrounding the beast are observable to the dwellers on earth. That is why they "marvel to see" the beast. This is not a hidden event. With this in mind, we now face another issue. The ESV, NIV and RSV make another emendation that changes more of the meaning. Rather than translating the verb and the noun as *singular* (as the NASB does), these translations provide a *plural* rendition. They translate "whose *names* have not been written" (my emphasis). This makes the verse read as if there are *specific, individual* names in this book. But if this is true, these *names* written in the book of life from before the foundation of the world are entirely hidden from human apprehension. This stands in opposition to the emphasis of this verse on observable reality, not hidden lists. So how can the translators justify the plural "names"?

Furthermore, one must question the idea that "the name not written" means names of specific individuals since this concept is not prominent in Hebrew thinking. Hebrew thinking is communal. It views those who are God's children *as a whole*. Thus, "*all Israel* will be saved" is not about individuals of Jewish origin. It is about the totality of those who follow YHWH designated by "Israel." Perhaps "name not written in the book" has the same communal application, i.e., all those *as a whole* who are not His children, not specific individuals.

These problems allow us to suggest that the phrase "from the foundation of the world" could be applied to the beast. Its *name* (singular) is not written in the book. In fact, given the fluidity of Greek positioning, the singular noun and verb here are more likely to modify the singular *therion* (beast) than the plural fabrication of "names." But there are more issues than this. The Greek pronoun *hos* (whose – as in "whose name") is plural. This would lead us to believe that "whose" refers to "earth dwellers." But "name" (*onoma*) is still singular regardless of the plural *hos*. So is the associated verb, *gegraptai* (third person, perfect passive, singular). Perhaps we are faced with the Hebraic idea of a name *as a community*, not as individuals.

Even if we resolve this additional problem, we are still faced with the issue of the identity of the beast. End-times advocates make attempts to identify the beast as something or someone. But behind this interpretation is a presupposition about the structure of time. The Greek idea of time is linear. Events happen once and are never repeated in the same way that points on a line are sequential. If John's vision employs a Greek view of time, then the arrival of the beast occurs at a specific point in the timeline of human history. The beast has a unique "name" identifying its existence on the time line. But the Hebrew view of time is not linear. It is a cycloidal curve, the path traced out by a point on the circumference of a circle as it travels along a surface. Think about a tire rolling down a hill with a red dot at one point on the circumference. Then follow the path of the dot. From a Hebraic perspective, the presence of the beast is concomitant with the creation of Mankind. As long as there have been dwellers on earth, the beast has been with us. That the beast is manifest in some fuller way at some further point does not entail that there was no beast prior to this manifestation. It simply entails that we now observe the evidence of the existence of the beast in a new way. In fact, we might argue that the phrase "was and is not and is to come" is a deliberate allusion to the same continual but hidden presence of Yeshua, who was (before the foundation of the earth), was not (observed to die) and is to come (will return), perhaps to indicate that the pattern of the beast mimics the pattern of the Christ. If we read the text this way, then modifying "dwellers of earth" with "from the foundation of the world" simply indicates that *since the creation of Man* the character of the beast has been present. The serpent was in the Garden *before* we got there.

The conclusion is this: If Revelation 17:8 is used as justification for moving the prepositional phrase in Revelation 13:8, then the theologian must demonstrate that there can be only one reading of the location of the phrase in 17:8, namely, as a modifier of "name." But an analysis of 17:8 demonstrates that there are *multiple* valid readings of this text, none of which violates the context nor the ethos of Hebraic thinking. And since the prepositional phrase cannot be firmly attached only to "name," we must question the affirmation that it must be attached to "names" in Revelation 13:8. In the end, there is still no linguistic reason to not to read the verse as it appears in the Greek text, "the Lamb slain before the foundation of the world."

The Hebrew Background

Katabole is translated by two different Hebrew words, *yasad* and *kun*. We looked at these briefly in our opening discussion of *katabole*, but now we need to dig deeper.

yasad – to establish, to found, to lay a foundation (TWOT 875) S3245 TDOT Vol VI, pp. 109-121.

yasad is used to describe laying a foundation of a building or city, founding the earth, or an appointment or ordination of a person to a task or position. Its derivatives are:

yesud – foundation, beginning
yesod – foundation, base (of the altar), principles upon which people are to build their lives (*yesudah* – Psalm 87:1 – Jerusalem the permanent place of His dwelling
musad – foundation
mosad – foundation

Significant verses employing *yasad* or its derivatives are:

> Ezra 3:12
> 1 Kings 16:34
> Psalm 119:152
> Proverbs 10:25
> Isaiah 28:16 (cf. Romans 9:33 and 1 Peter 2:6)
> Haggai 2:18
> Zechariah 8:9

There is only one occurrence of *yasad* in the Pentateuch (Exodus 9:18). The word is equally distributed in Psalms and Isaiah, but there are very few occurrences in the rest of the prophets. It is used far less than the other Hebrew equivalent, *kun*.

The Hebrew word *yasad* describes the physical reality of the base of a building or structure and is used metaphorically for the foundation of such things as human existence, the earth and the code of conduct from human behavior. Some important nuances must be noted in this metaphorical usage. First, *yasad* describes something *permanent*. It is not used for temporary structures or for transitional ways of life. The idea behind *yasad* is its focus on stability and permanence rather than on the actual structure or concept (such as human existence) itself. For this reason, *yasad* can refer to the commandments themselves and the foundation and creation of the earth. Permanence and unalterability are captured in *yasad*.

However, there are instances where this basic meaning, "what is permanent, stable and reliable," is not present. In these cases, the word contrasts what is "below" from what is "above" or what is "first" instead of "last." Perhaps there is a connection between this usage of the word and the mystical level of PaRDeS, *sod*, for what is *sod* is "below" all the other levels of interpretation and is hidden from view.

What is important for an inquiry into the Hebraic background is the connection of *yasad* to the context of sacrifice. The noun *yesod* is used in connection with the propitiatory consecration of the altar and with the sin offering (Leviticus 4:7, 18, 25, 30, 34; Exodus 30:10; Leviticus 16:18f; and Ezekiel 43:20). After the priest places the blood of the ritual sacrifice on the horns of the altar and sprinkles it on the side of the altar, he is to pour out the remainder on the base (*yesod*) of the altar. Any Jew in the first century would have recognized this element of the ritual and would have known that *yesod* (foundation – base) was intimately connected to sacrifice.

The further derivative, *mosad*, makes another connection between the Messiah and the altar. *Mosadot* (plural) is the word used in Jeremiah 51:26 to describe the commandment of God that no stone from Babylon will be used as a foundation (*mosadot*) for any of God's purposes. Babylon is to be laid waste. Isaiah employs the same word in the passage concerning YHWH's supreme authority and His unassailable charity with regard to Israel and Jacob (Isaiah 40:21-27). In Isaiah 58:1-12 the word describes the cosmic consequences of repentance and subsequent acts of righteousness. Once the people act in Torah obedience, "those from among you will rebuild the ancient ruins; you will raise up the age-old foundations" (Isaiah 58:12). YHWH's promise of restoration is extended by Jeremiah. "If the heavens above can be measured and the foundations (*mosadot*) of the earth searched out below, then I will also cast off all the offspring of Israel" (Jeremiah 31:37). The impact of this ironic prophetic announcement is the *eternal and irreplaceable* covenant between YHWH and Israel. Once again we find the nuances of utter reliability and permanence in the *ysd* root.

Further consideration must be given to the evidence that *yasad* describes the "activity as a whole," not simply the resulting event or condition.[35] This implies that *yasad* carries the sense of purposeful continuation to completion. As an example, the use of *yasad* in Psalm 104:8 implies that YHWH is actively preparing a place and that this activity results in the intended goal, rather than simply

---

[35] Cf. R. Mosis, *yasad*, TDOT, Vol. VI, p. 115.

stating that such a place was appointed by YHWH. Other examples confirm the *process toward final objective* found underlying *yasad*. This is particularly important in verses that speak about YHWH's act of creation. The sense of *yasad* does not focus the reader on the resulting final event (the creation) but rather on the One who brought it about as a purposeful action (the Creator). In other words, the emphasis is not on what was produced in creation but rather on the stability, reliability and permanence of the *actor*, the one who caused the result. For example, Psalm 102:25 uses *yasad* to describe not the earth but the One who founded the earth. It is God's character that remains permanently the same and this permanence is exhibited in His creation. "Thus none of the creation passages involving *ysd* speaks of a prior act of creation; all describe Yahweh, present either speaking or addressed, as the one who founded the earth and stretched out the heavens, i.e., created the cosmos and its order."[36]

Finally, we should note the epistemological consequences associated with *yasad*. Because the foundations of the cosmos are laid out prior to any human experience, their precise specification and construction is unavailable and unknowable to men. "Before the foundations" implies that such knowledge cannot be attained by human kind. This is the background of the personification of Wisdom in Proverbs 3. YHWH founds the earth by wisdom. Wisdom existed in personified form *before* the creation. Therefore, only YHWH and Wisdom have accessibility to the understanding of the

---

[36] R. Mosis, *yasad*, TDOT, Vol. VI, p. 118.

beginnings of the cosmos. "Only in part and only indirectly can one gain the wisdom that belongs completely and directly to Yahweh alone, which is found in his work of creation."[37] The time and place of the foundation story about Man is "reserved to Yahweh alone."[38]

kun – to bring into being, to establish as a certainty (TWOT 964) S3559 TDOT Vol. VII, pp. 89-101. To cause to stand in an upright position, to fix or establish, make steadfast.

Derivatives:

ken – right, true, "yes", correct, "thus"
makon – place, as "to put in place"
tekuna – fashion, as "to fashion or make"

Examples of *kun* and its derivatives can be found in:

> Genesis 41:32
> Exodus 8:26
> Psalm 5:9
> Psalm 8:3
> Psalm 97:2
> 2 Samuel 7:13
> Deuteronomy 32:6
> Proverbs 8:27
> Deuteronomy 13:14
> 1 Samuel 23:23

The word occurs only sixteen times in the Pentateuch. The majority of the occurrences are in

---

[37] *Ibid.*
[38] *Ibid.*, p. 119.

Psalms and Proverbs where it is used most often metaphorically.

"Yahweh is frequently the subject, a sign that the verb denotes an exceptionally effective act."[39] The basic meaning of the word is "to prepare, to make ready" but in the polel it means "to establish, to make permanent." Koch points out that noun forms are rare. The singular is always only about holy places. The plural is found only in Psalm 104:5 (foundations of the earth). Koch concludes that this evidence "points to a lexeme denoting energetic, purposeful action, aimed at forming useful enduring places and institutions, with a secondary element asserting the reliability of statements. . . it must be noted, however, that the focus in most texts is not on a state, but rather on making or becoming. What is emphasizes is not stability but permanence and utility. If we try to reduce the various usages to a single common denominator, it would be: 'call something into being in such a way that it fulfills its function (in the life of an individual, in society, or in the cosmos) independently and permanently.'"[40]

The word reflects the character of God revealed in the Genesis account of creation. It suggests "the power of an ordered and orderly reality."[41] Koch notes that we rarely find its derivative, *ken*, in descriptions of ordinary life. This is unusual since the word expresses effectual action. The reason for this unique quality of *ken* (*kun*) may be that it has strong connections with the ritual preparation of

---

[39] K. Koch, *kun, ken, makon, mekona, tekuna*, TDOT, Vol. VII, p. 89.
[40] *Ibid.*, p. 93.
[41] *Ibid.*, p. 94.

sacrifices, and is therefore associated with the efficacious nature of God's acts rather than the acts of men. This is derived from "the conviction that cultic acts are the source of all life and prosperity for those who share in the cult. Therefore creative, purposeful preparation is necessary, on the part of God as well as the worshipper, to guarantee the success of the rite."[42]

In the verbal form, *hekin*, the word "is never used of creation as a whole, but of extraordinary works that bring beneficent order to the rest of creation."[43] Once again we see the word's connection with divine action.

One other form of the word *ken* is significant for our inquiry. *Nakon me'az* connects the Davidic kingdom on earth with a divine kingship in heaven (Psalm 93:2, Psalm 96:10, 1 Chronicles 16:30). The translation of this phrase ("from then on") expresses the permanence of this relationship. Psalm 89:15 and 97:2 describe righteousness and justice as the enduring foundations (*makon*) of the divine throne.

John Oswalt notes five related meanings of *kun*.[44] First, although rare the word sometimes means simply to bring something into being. Secondly, a large number of occurrences mean "to prepare," in the sense of anticipating something that will happen in the future. This group of uses is often associated with preparing for sacrifices, preparing hearts to be receptive to the Lord or preparing for God's actions.

[42] *Ibid.*, p. 96.
[43] *Ibid.*, p. 97.
[44] John Oswalt, *kun*, TWOT, Vol. 1, pp. 432-434

God Himself prepares for future eventualities including both creative and judicial acts. Thirdly, Oswalt notes that some uses of *kun* seem to fluctuate between "prepare" and "establish." God's creative acts describe what He prepares, and at the same time what is established; for example, Proverbs 8:27 and Proverbs 3:19. What is important is that this language is the language of royalty. In this sense, it has a kind of permanence. Fourthly, twenty-five times the word is used about establishing a dynasty, most often as a direct result of God's appointment of the line of a king. This, of course, leads directly to establishing the kingdom of the Messiah. Oswalt comments, "But the great test of God's kingship is the problem of sin. This problem is dealt with through the establishment of a people (Deut 32:6). The particular creation language of this verse is significant. Redemption is a part of the total work of creation. Furthermore, God overcomes sin by establishing his sanctuary in the midst of his people (Ex 15:17; Isa 2:2)."[45]

Finally, the fifth use of *kun* is the sense of well-being as a result of abiding under the authority of God. This usage is found in verses like Psalm 112:7 (a heart fixed upon the Lord). Here the word includes the idea of permanence that results in confidence.

---

[45] Oswalt, J. N. (1999). 964 כון. In R. L. Harris, G. L. Archer, Jr. & B. K. Waltke (Eds.), *Theological Wordbook of the Old Testament* (R. L. Harris, G. L. Archer, Jr. & B. K. Waltke, Ed.) (electronic ed.) (433). Chicago: Moody Press.

Let's examine some of the occurrences of this word that bear on our inquiry into the phrase "before the foundation of the world."

Genesis 41:32 *Now as for the repeating of the dream to Pharaoh twice, it means that the matter is determined by God, and God will quickly bring it about.* NASB

In this verse, the word *nakon* (from *kun*) is the verbal form "to prepare, to make ready, to erect, to set up, to fix, to determine." From the context we see that the customary meaning, "to bring something into being so much that it is established as a certainty" applies. Here God guarantees the reality portrayed in Pharaoh's dream. Pharaoh can act on the dream because the circumstances it reveals will come to pass. For our purposes, we should note that the word describes conditions that cannot be altered, once they are established. Here *kun* points to permanence, a nuance that is especially important when the word is applied to divine actions taken before the foundation of the world.

Exodus 8:26 *But Moses said, "It is not right to do so, for we will sacrifice to the Lord our God what is an abomination to the Egyptians.* NASB

The same Hebrew verbal form (*nakon*) is used in this verse to describe what is proper or correct. What is established as true under the direction of YHWH also implies correct action. It is not sufficient to merely assent to the truth of the proposition. In Hebrew thought, cognitive truth entails behavioral commitment. For our investigation, the use of *kun* to describe what is fixed before the foundation of the world is not simply a theological idea. Behavior is implied. Some action is taken, and that action has consequences for the rest of creation.

Psalm 5:9 *There is nothing reliable in what they say; Their inward part is destruction itself. Their throat is an open grave; They flatter with their tongue.* NASB

The NASB translates *nekonah* as "reliable," connecting this word to the Hebrew concept of truth. Here we find a nuance of *kun* that leads us to the connection with what is established by God. The psalmist portrays the wicked as totally unreliable (untruthful) and as a result subject to destruction.

Psalm 8:3 *When I consider Your heavens, the work of Your fingers, The moon and the stars, which You have ordained;* NASB

Here the verb *kun* is translated "ordained" ("set in place" – ESV). Once more we see that the connection of *kun* to divine actions entails their permanence whether that enduring character is ascribed to physical reality or divine instructions. Even the stars and the moon confirm the utter reliability and continuity of YHWH. Notice that the psalmist considers the heavens as "Your work" – that is, God's ownership is fixed in His creativity.

We should notice the recurring theme of perpetual immutability. What God prepares and establishes and ordains remains forever. For our inquiry, proclamations concerning the sacrifice of the Lamb before the foundation of the world imply that this sacrifice is permanent. It does not need to be repeated, in fact, it cannot be repeated since what it brings into being remains in place forever.

Psalm 97:2 *Clouds and thick darkness surround Him; Righteousness and justice are the foundation of His throne.* NASB

The element of permanence is also expressed in this description of YHWH's relationship to righteousness and justice. They are permanent attributes. Unlike the false gods of pagan cultures, YHWH is not fickle or subject to persuasion. His standard of holiness applied to all, with equal measure, governs all His actions toward the creation. We find the same idea of permanence even when the word is used to describe earthly kingdoms that are set in place by God. The permanence of the dynasty is not accounted for by the kings themselves, or any actions they might take. It is accounted for because the kingdoms rest on God's faithfulness. Thus, we find in 2 Samuel 7:13 (*He shall build a house for my name, and I will establish the throne of his kingdom forever.* ESV) a proclamation that the eternal nature of the Davidic line has been set in place by YHWH, not David.

God's actions with permanent consequence even apply to Israel itself. Moses says, *"Do you thus repay the Lord, O foolish and unwise people? Is not He your Father who has bought you? He has made you and established you"* (Deuteronomy 32:6 NASB). Israel's permanence as the chosen people of God does not depend on their behavior, before or after YHWH's selection. It is YHWH's action alone that establishes the permanence of Israel. The eternal character of Israel and its role in the scheme of God's redemptive plan is independent of Israel's actual obedience or disobedience. While it is true that Israel's disobedience can frustrate the orderly procession of God's purposes, such disobedience cannot erase those purposes. Use of the verb *kun* implies that God's selection of Israel is as immutable as His characteristics of righteousness and justice.

This element affects our understanding of the event of the Lamb slain before the foundation of the world. If the Lamb is slain before the foundation of the world, the implication is that *this* action, not the crucifixion, is the place of atonement – an atonement that has eternal consequences and permanence. Proverbs 8:27[46] suggests that personified Wisdom was equally present when the heavens were established. Since the New Testament connects personified Wisdom with the Messiah, first-century followers of the Way could have drawn the conclusion that the Messiah's role in forgiveness was also present when the heavens were established. Certainly John would have considered this connection in his opening prologue.

Deuteronomy 13:14 *then you shall investigate and search out and inquire thoroughly. If it is true and the matter established that this abomination has been done among you,* NASB

---

[46] "When he established the heavens, I was there; when he drew a circle on the face of the deep," Proverbs 8:27 ESV

1 Samuel 23:23 *So look, and learn about all the hiding places where he hides himself and return to me with certainty, and I will go with you; and if he is in the land, I will search him out among all the thousands of Judah.* NASB

These last two verses in our investigation point out that *kun* can communicate that idea of certainty. In other verses, the matter to be examined or reported must be vouched as entirely truthful, i.e., certain.

From this brief investigation of the Hebrew words behind the Greek *katabole*, we can draw the following conclusions with regard to the issue of the sacrificial atonement:

1. The Hebrew background places emphasis on the permanence of events described by *kun* and *yasad*. In these cases, YHWH is most often the guarantor of the eternal character of the action or event.
2. Both words describe the perpetual immutability of YHWH's actions. As verbs employed to recount the sacrifice in the heavenly Temple, these verbs would have conveyed a "once for all time" idea.
3. We should also notice that these verbs imply the unimpeachable character of YHWH, His inscrutable methods, the eternal nature of His covenants and the resulting well-being of His actions. At every turn, the use of *yasad* or *kun* emphasizes the singularity of the event and its results.

themelios – Additional Greek Considerations

The second Greek word translated "foundation" is *themelios*. We will examine the use of *themelios* in the following verses:

> 1 Corinthians 3:12
> Ephesians 2:20
> 1 Corinthians 3:11
> 1 Timothy 6:19
> Revelation 21:14
> 1 Peter 5:10
> 2 Timothy 2:19
> Hebrew 6:1
> Hebrew 11:10
> Revelation 21:19

1 Corinthians 3:12 *Now if anyone builds on the foundation with gold, silver, precious stones, wood, hay, straw* ESV

The word *themelios* is used both literally (foundation or foundation stone of a building) and figuratively (Christ is the foundation). The theological element is present in the description of the Messiah and the apostles as the foundation of the followers of the Way. Believers are encouraged to build upon this foundation. Clearly the New Testament authors have the role and position of Yeshua as Messiah in mind. No other foundation is possible for those who are part of the Messianic community. To build on this foundation is to obey His commandments, making Him Lord of life. We should notice the critical connection between life, obedience and Lordship, often associated with "foundation."

Ephesians 2:20 *built on the foundation of the apostles and prophets, Christ Jesus himself being the cornerstone*

Paul addresses believing Gentiles. Because of God's grace through Yeshua, they are no longer "stranger and aliens" (Ephesians 3:19) but now fellow-citizens. He then provides the reason for this transferred status. ". . . having been built upon the foundation of the apostles and prophets, Yeshua HaMashiach being the cornerstone." Our investigation concerns the two words *themelios* (foundation) and *akrogoniaios* (cornerstone). The allusions are clearly to passages in the Tanakh, particularly those in Isaiah 28 (*yesod*), indicating that in addition to the literal definition (basic stone of a building) the figurative usage implies confirmation, stability and reliability of principles or actions.

With the same metaphorical usage found in Corinthians, Paul extends the concept to include the prophets, probably because he views the ministry of Yeshua as the fulfillment of prophetic claims. This time, Paul describes the relationship between the apostles, prophets and the Messiah as the relationship between the entire foundation and the cornerstone. Paul may have the words of Isaiah in mind. Isaiah 28:16-17 reveals that God laid a foundation (*yasad*) additionally described by two Hebrew words, *'eben* (stone) and *pennah* (cornerstone). We noticed the same combination in

Jeremiah 51:26.[47] Through Jeremiah, God tells us that no stone (*lemosedot* – actually " no stones") from Babylon will *ever* be the *'eben lepinna* (stone of the corner). What does this mean?

Mosis observes "*mosedot* cannot denote the act of laying a foundation; it must refer to the actual foundations. . . . The notion of 'foundations on which the structure as a whole is built' is then extended to the structure of the cosmos."[48] The corner stone of the cosmos is Yeshua, but this does not simply mean Yeshua, the man, the Messiah, who walked the earth. It means the pre-incarnate, incarnate, exalted Messiah who will rule and reign visibly as He already does invisibly; and that also means the *character and actions* of the revealed Messiah. We have the tendency to think only of the salvation message as this corner stone, but anyone who realizes that He is King of all must recognize that this corner stone includes *all* His thoughts, words and deeds. In the ancient world, every act of the King was a telling sign of the King's expectations for his subjects. Every thought and every word of the King was crucially important. Yeshua's kingdom is no different.

1 Corinthians 3:11 *no one can lay a foundation other than that which is laid, which is Yeshua HaMashiach.*

Here Paul emphasizes the uniqueness, primacy and superiority of the "foundation" provided in Yeshua.

---

[47] *They will not take from you even **a stone for the corner** nor a stone for foundations, but you will be desolate forever,"* *declares the LORD.* Jeremiah 51:26 NASB

[48] R. Mosis, *yasad*, TDOT, Vol. VI, p. 113.

But there is no temporal indication that this was done at the cross. In fact, if Paul views the foundation in Hebraic terms, then the whole scope of Yeshua's existence is in mind; and considering Paul's perspective from Philippians 2:6-8, the scope of the work of Yeshua must extend to His pre-incarnate existence. The foundation was laid at the moment Yeshua volunteered to empty Himself. That certainly did not take place at the moment of His earthly conception nor did it take place when He was lifted on the cross. Once again we encounter a Hebraic concept that sees the *result* of an act latent within the *origin* of the act. Divine intention *is* divine execution. Greek can separate the two as though they are distinct components, but Hebrew does not view them in this way. The consequences of sin are inherent and active within the act of sin. Punishment is not a separately applied element. Just so, the incarnation is not a separate event from the determination to provide redemption. Its *manifestation* may appear temporally separate from its source, but it is one continuous act, from intention to final glorification (yet to come).

1 Timothy 6:19 *"storing up for themselves the treasure of a good foundation for the future"*

Paul exhorts Timothy to teach the wealthy that riches will not provide them with what matters most in life. Since God is the source of one's earthly assets, we must look to Him as the provider and sustainer, not to the accumulation of wealth here. Paul's perspective is that the treasure for future life is accumulated in being rich in good works and generous with what God provides. This is both

Scriptural and rabbinic. Here the Greek word *themelios* (foundation) is used to describe the underlying supporting structure of the treasure that God values.

Revelation 21:14 *"and the wall of the city had twelve foundation stones,"* is a clear allusion to the Twelve Tribes, now called the Twelve apostles of the Lamb. This description of the city of God in the new heaven draws from Israel's history with God. Here the Greek word is directly related to Old Testament roots.

1 Peter 5:10 *"and after you have suffered for a little, the God of all grace, who called you in His eternal glory in Christ, will Himself perfect, confirm, strengthen and establish you."*

The Greek verb, *themelioo*, is translated "establish" in this verse. Clearly associated with the idea of laying a foundation, here the word carries the nuance of making one's footing (life) secure. Peter's context is tribulation. In the midst of persecution, believers are to remember that their suffering is only temporary because God's purposes still prevail. Such suffering leads to God's promise to make His children complete, to vouch for them as His own, to strengthen them in their walk and to provide a foundation that will not fail.

2 Timothy 2:19 *"Nevertheless, the firm foundation of God stands, bearing this seal: 'The Lord knows those who are his,' and 'Let every one who names the name of the Lord abstain from wickedness.'"*

Reflect on this verse from the first century perspective of Paul. What would Paul consider the "firm foundation of God"? How would Timothy have understood these words? It is obvious that neither Paul nor Timothy could have understood "the firm foundation of God" as New Testament teaching, for the New Testament as we know it did not exist when Paul wrote this. To suggest that the firm foundation of God is restricted to the words of Yeshua ignores the fact that Timothy only knows these words if they have been transmitted to him orally. But Paul's use of *themelios* cannot mean an oral rendering, even if the words are transmitted correctly (rabbinic expectation of memorized transmission). The *Exegetical Dictionary of the New Testament*, notes that Pauline use of *themelios* is metaphorical. It is "the building of the community and its teaching ('system of instruction')."[49] Paul deliberately states that he will not build on the foundation of another (Romans 15:20) but on the one foundation, Yeshua HaMashiach (1 Corinthians 3:10-12). Paul expands this thought in Ephesians 2:20 where the apostles and the prophets are included in the firm foundation. G. Petzke, in the *Exegetical Dictionary of the New Testament*, claims that this verse views the "Church itself" as the firm foundation, but this claim is unwarranted since no "church" existed when Paul wrote this letter to Timothy. Furthermore, Paul admonished Timothy to remain faithful to the same "sincere faith within you which first dwelt in your grandmother Lois, and your mother Eunice." This reference must indicate the faith of God-fearing Gentile women who were part

---

[49] *Exegetical Dictionary of the New Testament*, Vol. 2, p. 139

96

of the Messianic community. Since there is no biblical justification to suggest that this community departed from the standard of Torah, it would be impossible to claim that Paul *substituted* the Church for Torah. If Paul remained Torah-observant, and god-fearing Gentiles were expected to learn Torah in the Messianic community, it is anachronistic to claim that Paul has the "Church" in mind in this verse.

Hebrew 6:1 *"Therefore let us leave the elementary doctrine of Christ and go on to maturity, not laying again a foundation of repentance from dead works and of faith toward God,"* ESV

What are we to make of this statement? Is the author of Hebrews telling us that we need to move on from the simple ideas of Yeshua, never to repeat a previously-laid foundation of "works" and "faith" toward God? Does he mean that we should progress *past* Yeshua's *introductory* thought as if it no longer has value for the mature believer? Does he suggest that Yeshua's simple doctrine of repentance must be put behind us as we grow spiritually? And what does he mean by "repentance from dead works"? Does that mean, as most Christians read it, that the "law" doesn't count anymore – that the "law" is associated with "dead works"?

Answering these questions requires some serious study of the Greek text. Unfortunately, for most of us, that means the answers are hidden from view. We have to rely on the expertise of others and that usually means we are subject to the bias and theological presuppositions of the experts. So we

97

must proceed carefully, constantly asking, "Why does the translator say this? What would this have meant to the first-century reader, especially to the first-century *Jewish* (Messianic or otherwise) reader (since the letter to the Hebrews presupposes an audience familiar with all kinds of Jewish thought and customs)?"

Let's start with the idea of "the elementary doctrine of Christ." The author of Hebrews instructs us to "leave" this. The Greek verb is *aphiemi*, "to send away, to go, to release, to give up, to let go." The noun almost always means "forgiveness," where the idea is "to pardon." It is found throughout the gospels. Forgiveness is a central theme of Yeshua's message and while it may seem simple, it is hardly "elementary" in the sense that it can be later cast aside. Without it, nothing else happens. Since the author of the letter is exhorting his readers to become mature in their understanding and practice, his emphasis is not on abandoning prior teaching but rather on building upon it so that the believer does not get stuck in the first steps of the process. It is noteworthy that *aphiemi* is *not* used in Hebrews for forgiveness, as it is in the gospels. This means that we can't understand the meaning of *aphiemi* until we resolve the question about what is *elementary doctrine*?

That expression is *arches Christou logon*. But this presents a translation problem. Literally it is "beginning Christ's words." Does it mean "the words spoken by Christ" or does it mean "the spoken word about Christ"? Furthermore, does it refer to those words spoken during His ministry on earth, or does it refer to the general teaching about the Messiah, or does it refer to the eschatological Christ, the exalted King? The ESV, NASB and NIV translation of *arches* as "elementary" could lead us to think that whatever this "doctrine" is, it is simple and suitable only for the less-informed, the simple. But that places an artificial value on the meaning of the text. The Greek word, *arche*, means "beginning, first, ancient, foundational." Procreation is the beginning of life on earth, but it isn't "simple." It is foundational. It is first. But one would hardly argue that it is elementary in the sense that it is suitable only for simple people. If that were the case, we would have no hesitation at all telling the youngest child how we came to be. We must read this word, *arches*, as "basic, first, foundational," not as "simple, that is, of no ultimate value."

The ESV needlessly complicates the problem by translating *Christou logon* (the words of Christ or the words about Christ) as "doctrine." In our culture, "doctrine" carries the nuance of inflexible dogma, a final and complete statement of a Scriptural truth. One does *not* leave doctrines behind. To do so is tantamount to heresy; but if we stick to the direct meaning of the expression *Christou logon*, then we have either "the words of Christ" or "the words about Christ." Either choice shifts us away from the idea that we are to let go of a doctrine. Now the focus must be on these words, not the theological propositions found in these words.

This should help us decide what the author means. If his point is to move beyond the first words of Yeshua (or about Yeshua), then we see that he is not advocating abandoning the teaching in those words, but rather *building up them*. In this sense, the foundation words of Yeshua bring us peace with God because they offer us true forgiveness. But this is only the *first* step in our relationship. We are not intended to stay there. We are to "press on" (*pheromentha* – "to bear, i.e. to produce, to carry, to bring forth) toward maturity. Certainly we cannot bear fruit of righteousness by abandoning the words of Yeshua. We must take those words as the foundation for further development. We must bring forth what the words imply, that is, maturity, to move beyond the first step of repentance and forgiveness toward the full implementation of Yeshua's calling. Given the context of the previous chapter, this must be clear. Remaining followers who claim nothing more than being forgiven is not the intention or the program of Yeshua. We are called to more than that. We can't get going until we have taken that step, but to stay there is to defeat the entire purpose of forgiveness.

Now comes the contrast. Too often these words are taken as a declaration that "dead works" means the law is no longer in effect. Because we import a "law vs. grace" mentality, we read "dead works" as if it means "trying to be saved by doing what the law says." But no Jew would have understood these words in that way. The law doesn't bring death. It brings life! The Torah tells me how I am to live *after* I have peace with God through His grace. Paul argues as much in Romans. Only those who continued to claim that Gentiles had to become Jews (by certain actions for proselytes) in order to worship YHWH, are subject to this criticism. Paul's argument in Galatians definitively overturns the claim that we must *become Jewish* before we can enter into the covenant of God. But that does not set aside the Torah. It simply demonstrates that the Torah *is not about salvation.* It is about life after grace.

Then what does it mean to say, "not laying again a foundation of repentance from dead works"? Certainly we understand the idea of not going back again and again to the first step of repentance. While followers need to repent of sins as they align their lives with Yeshua's call, this is not the same as that first step of repentance, the step that puts us on the road toward conformity with the Son. John makes this clear in his first letter. But what is the connection to "dead works"? Ellingworth's comment of the introduction of this phrase is instructive. "The context requires [*themelio*n . . . *metanoias* . . .] to mean 'a foundation which consists of repentance . . ,' not, as more commonly, 'a foundation on which repentance et. are built.' The list contains nothing distinctively Christian, and of course nothing exclusively Jewish; such a sharp dichotomy is alien to a Jewish Christian writing mainly to readers in the same tradition."[50] The list follows in verse 2 and includes hand washing, laying on of hands, resurrection of the dead and eternal punishment.

If you subscribe to the Christian idea of replacement theology (that God has, in the *new dispensation*, replaced Israel and the law with the church and the message of grace), then you are likely to read this as

---

[50] Paul Ellingworth, *The Epistle to the Hebrews*, NIGTC, 1993, p. 313.

an indictment of Torah. You will think of Torah as "dead works." But the perspective of Paul, and even the author of Hebrews, must cause us to reject this false dichotomy. For any follower of the Way in the first century, Torah is still the living, guiding instruction necessary for fulfilling the purposes of God on earth. To abandon Torah is to abandon faith in YHWH. Many significant scholars today are realizing that the prior teaching of the Church regarding replacement theology is mistaken. And we can confidently assert that no one reading this letter in the first century would have believed that the Church *replaced* Israel as God's elect or that grace *set aside* Torah.

"Dead works" is an expression found only in Hebrews. Ellingworth notes that the parallel with *pistis* (faith in the living God) "requires the stronger meaning 'works which lead to death.'"[51] The contrast is not with works (law) and grace, but rather with human behaviors that lead to death versus those that lead to life. Paul makes a point of this in Galatians 5, but the echo goes back to Moses in Deuteronomy 30:19 ("I have set before you today life and death . . . Now choose life"). If this is the echo of the author, then he clearly cannot mean the Torah is no longer valid. Moses' entire exhortation is built on the premise that *Torah is life*! It is important to note that the author never develops this theme. He simply *assumes* that the reader will hear the echo of Moses and know what is required.

---

[51] Paul Ellingworth, *The Epistle to the Hebrews*, NIGTC, 1993, p. 314.

As far as our examination of "foundation" (*themelios*) is concerned, here we find the word used in direct connection with the once-given revelation of YHWH. Torah reveals the way of life. Torah also reveals the consequences of not following this way. Death! This foundation, established by God Himself, remains the permanent and eternal expression of God's will for men. *Themelios* retains the character of the Hebrew *yasad* and *kun*.

Hebrews 11:10 *For he was looking forward to the city that has foundations, whose designer and builder is God.* ESV

In contrast to the wandering life of Abraham, the city of God is permanent. The English translations omit the definite article in Greek (*the* foundations) that may indicate emphasis, underscoring the stark contrast with the nomadic Abraham. As the author of Hebrews later implies, this is the heavenly city, the other Yerushalayim (itself a plural noun). "The implication here, and in vv. 14-16, is that Abraham and the other patriarchs were seeking a city which, because it was in heaven, was not yet (v.7; cf. v.3) visible to them, but which (like God's 'resting place' in 3:7-4:11) has existed from the beginning of creation, and may indeed be anticipated now in worship (12:22)."[52] Once again we see that *themelios* is an adequate substitute for the Hebraic idea of divine permanence and immutable execution of YHWH's will.

---

[52] Paul Ellingworth, *The Epistle to the Hebrews*, NIGTC, 1993, p. 585.

Revelation 21:19 *The foundation stones of the city wall were adorned with every kind of precious stone. The first foundation stone was jasper; the second, sapphire; the third, chalcedony; the fourth, emerald;* NASB

Our final look at *themelios* shows its use in a purely physical context – here as the description of the base of the city wall. While some theologians may attempt to find allegory in this description, it is the nature of apocalyptic literature to use vague symbols so that the text remains applicable across the ages. What John actually had in mind we may never know, but we can certainly appreciate the fact that "foundation" has more than spiritual and metaphorical meaning.

What conclusions can we draw from our examination of both the Hebrew and Greek vocabulary translated "foundation"? Perhaps the summary takes us back to the Hebrew idea of permanence. Behind the Greek words lies this Hebrew base. What God does has eternal consequence. It is the temporal perspective of eternity that provides the insight into "foundation." In Hebrew thought the meaning of an event is often found in the fuller manifestation of that event. For example, while we have some understanding of the Kingdom of Heaven now, the full meaning of this concept will not become evident *until* or even *after* the return of the King, from our perspective, but the true meaning of "Kingdom of Heaven" is already a reality for YHWH because its full reality is an expression of His will. The temporal occurrences associated with the revelation of the Kingdom are *incidental* to its truth.

In like manner, the use of *yasad*, *kun*, *katabole* and *themelios* carry the same incidental temporality as icing on the cake of God's permanent covenant execution. The actions may seem temporally distinguishable for us, but from God's perspective, they are uniquely incorporated. God always *starts* what He finishes.

What does this tell us about the event of the *cross*? First, it removes the claim that the cross exists as an independent action in the divine purposes. Secondly, it suggests that the cross event is a *manifestation* of something that has been in process since before the foundation of the world. Thirdly, we find that there seems to be no justification for displacing the atonement from "before the foundation of the world" except theological bias. And finally, we have discovered that Hebrew thought provides a different view of the reality of manifestations of God's purposes – a view that does not easily mesh with our linear picture of time.

Now we need to examine the associated verses.

Chapter Three

The Blood

And according to the Law, one may almost say, all things are cleansed with blood, and without the shedding of blood there is no forgiveness. Hebrews 9:22 NASB

Re-examining our thinking about the sacrificial blood of Jesus will be difficult. To even suggest an alternative understanding of what we are about to investigate may cause apoplectic theological shock. Some may need to visit a therapist (as one of my undergraduate students once told me about his experience in a class I taught). But be assured that I am not taking you anywhere I have not gone, nor would I pretend that I haven't also spent a few hours with my theological therapy group.

The opening premise is unquestionable (at least we think so). "Without the shedding of blood there is no forgiveness." What could be more fundamental than that? Built upon the solid rock of the proleptic sacrificial system, we find this idea asserted over and over in Christian thought and liturgy. "Washed by the blood" is such a ubiquitous theme in Christianity that none would raise any questions.

Except – except that Yeshua didn't offer His blood as a sacrifice on the cross. None of His blood was sprinkled on the altar. In fact, He wasn't even killed according to ritual practice. He wasn't executed by the priests. He wasn't crucified for religious apostasy (and if He were, it would be hard to see how He could be a ritual sacrifice). None of the blood of the Lamb touched any of the required places for the remission of sin. Nothing about the cross suggests that it meets the requirements necessary for forgiveness. Certainly Jewish believers would have known this. We might be separated from the direct and immediate connection between the altar, the sacrifice and forgiveness, but the author of Hebrews and his reading audience wasn't.

The thought is even more startling when we realize that this Greek verb (translated "shedding of blood") is only found in this one verse in the New Testament. *Hamatekchysia* only makes sense if it has a Hebraic connotation. The author of Hebrews goes to great lengths to assure that his readers understand that Yeshua is *the sacrifice* and that His blood does facilitate the forgiveness of sin. But it clearly doesn't happen on the cross.

Christian theologians are not unaware of this obvious difficulty. They suggest that it isn't *blood* that is necessary. What is necessary is *death*. "The point is that the giving of life is the necessary presupposition of forgiveness."[53] But this is a rationalization, not an exegesis. The entire cultus of Judaism taught, and still believes, that without the shedding of blood, sprinkled on the altar according to God's own instructions, there is no forgiveness. If the author of Hebrews is a Jew, and if Yeshua is a Jew, and if the readers are Jews, why would they ever conclude that *death* is the only requirement?

---

[53] J. Behm, *haima, haimatekchysia*, in TDNT (Abridged), p. 26.

This Christian re-interpretation makes it easy to avoid the issue of the altar, the temple and the sacrificial system, but it does so at the expense of violating everything taught about sacrifice in the Tanakh.

So, what do we do now? If the crucifixion is *not* the modus operandi of forgiveness, then how is forgiveness accomplished? Where is the blood of the Lamb sprinkled on the altar?

For the life of the flesh is in the blood, and I have given it for you on the altar to make atonement for your souls, for it is the blood that makes atonement by the life. Leviticus 17:11 ESV

As we have observed, Christian apologists often claim that the blood of Christ shed on the cross is the reason for the forgiveness of sin. Prior to Leon Morris' study of the concept of blood atonement,[54] some theologians referred to the claim that "life is in the blood" and therefore the cross represents atonement given via the life of Christ. But since Morris' study, this position has been untenable. Morris has conclusively demonstrated that in both the Old Testament and the New, the term "blood" is most commonly used to describe "death by violence," and this idea is paramount in its association with sacrifice. Morris shows that even the Leviticus passage (Leviticus 17:11) so often used as a proof text cannot be understood in the Hebraic worldview as a claim that life exists apart from physical blood. It is simply not possible to

---

[54] Leon Morris, *The Apostolic Preaching of the Cross* (Eerdmans, 1955), see in particular Chapter III, "The Blood."

think of the sacrifice as presenting "life" on the altar. "Blood shed stands, therefore, not for the release of life from the burden of the flesh, but for the bringing to an end of life in the flesh."[55] Morris points out the in Hebraic thought there is no immaterial existence of life apart from the body. This is why the Hebraic worldview has no concept of an immortal soul but rather looks for the resurrection of the *body* at the Day of Judgment.[56]

Atonement is not accomplished by offering *life* but rather by *giving up life*, and this is the meaning of "blood" in the sacrificial system. A blood sacrifice is a *death sacrifice*. But a blood sacrifice is *not* the only means of atonement available in the Hebraic worldview. Atonement may be achieved by anointing with oil (Leviticus 14:18), by offering incense (Numbers 16:46), through the scapegoat (Leviticus 16:10) and other means. When atonement involves the termination of life, even here it does not always demand a blood sacrifice. Atonement may be accomplished by "blotting out" a name from the Book of Life (Exodus 32:30-32), by zealous execution (Numbers 25:13), by delivering up enemies for proper punishment (2 Samuel 21:3 ff) and by slaying the red heifer (Deuteronomy 21:1-9). None of these *require* a blood (death) sacrifice although every one of them involves death in some sense or another. Morris concludes, "In each case it is the termination of life, the infliction of death that atones"[57] although the means by which death comes is quite different in each case. "[T]he evidence afforded by the use of

---

[55] Leon Morris, *The Apostolic Preaching of the Cross*, p. 113.
[56] Cf. Morris, p. 113.
[57] *op.cit.*, p. 115.

dam [blood] in the Old Testament indicates that it signifies life taken violently, rather than the continued presence of life available for some new function."[58]   Perhaps we must revise Abraham Heschel's evaluation of the difference between Judaism and Christianity. Heschel pointed out that Judaism is a religion focused on *life* whereas Christianity is a religion focused on *death*. But Morris' study demonstrates that the idea of death is not too far removed from the Hebraic worldview either. Death is a necessary component of sacrifice even if sacrifice is a necessary component of life with God.

Morris makes the observation that the use of blood in relation to Christ in the New Testament is predominately a circumlocution for the death of Yeshua. Morris notes, "[F]or a cross has no place in the sacrificial system, and stands only for a particularly unpleasant death."[59] The conclusion:

> Thus it seems tolerably certain that in both the Old and New Testaments the blood signifies essentially the death. It is freely admitted that there are some passages in which it is possible to interpret the blood as signifying life, but even these yield a better sense (and one which is consistent with the wider biblical usage), if understood to mean 'life given up in death'.[60]

Consider the impact that Morris' study has on theological claims like the one by Ridderbos, "the

---

[58] *op. cit.*, p. 117.
[59] *Ibid.*, p. 119.
[60] *Ibid.*, p. 122.

propitiatory sacrifice enters in substitutionally between the holy God and sinful man, because the life given up in the sacrifice through the attendant shedding of blood covers sin before the face of God and in this way atones."[61] If the blood refers not to giving up of life but rather to violent death, how are we to understand the idea of substitutionary atonement that is so much a part of Christian thinking? For now, perhaps it is enough just to ask, "Did I think that the blood was about *life* or about *death*?" Does this change our view about what is happening on the cross?

For it was the Father's good pleasure for all the fullness to dwell in Him, and through Him to reconcile all things to Himself, having made peace through the blood of His cross, through Him, I say, whether things on earth or things in heaven.
Colossians 1:19-20 NASB

If Morris is right and the idea of blood is about *death*, not life, then what about Paul's emphasis on the blood of Christ? Perhaps the place to start is with Paul's statement in Colossians 1:19-20. It is important to read exactly what this verse says, and not to read into the verse something it does not say. Notice the claim is *not* that *men* are reconciled to God through the death on the cross (for that is how we must understand "blood of His cross" after Morris). While men are included in this claim, the scope of the claim is much larger. *All* things, both on earth and in heaven, are reconciled. This claim is patently false if it applies only to sinful men since

---

[61] Herman Ridderbos, *Paul: An Outline of His Theology* (Eerdmans, 1975), p. 188.

there are no sinful men in heaven. Paul has in mind something far greater with the term *apokatallaxai*. The verb (*apokatallasso*) means "to make other than what it is, to alter, to change" and is often associated with monetary exchanges or substitutes. There is a subtlety involved in the use of this term, for the New Testament does not suggest that God is the object of reconciliation, as if He needs to be placated so as to divert His anger. The Scriptures claim that God Himself brings about this change in relationship. The object is "all things," including sinful men. Paul makes it clear that this change is the purpose of God brought about in the death of Yeshua (Romans 5:10). If it applies to *everything*, then it must be about more than our sins.

Notice that the result of this death on the cross is peace, not forgiveness. This makes perfect sense. Heaven and earth were not at peace because the purposes of God have not been fulfilled since the original act of disobedience. To bring peace to heaven and earth requires a *reunion* of God's design, a reconstitution of the original perfect creation where the will of the Father is perfectly executed on earth as it is in heaven. So while there is no doubt that God's purposes are fulfilled in heaven, the very fact that the creation has fallen into disobedience means that peace did not prevail until, as Paul suggests, the death of the Son on the cross. Ridderbos notes that Paul's statement does not mean a restoration of "the right disposition (e.g., among the apostate spirits), but rather of the divine government over all, through the fact, among other things, that the authority of the powers that have set themselves against God have been taken away and through Christ they have been subjected to God."[62] What is at stake on the stake is not expiation for sin but the re-establishment of *authority*! Paul reiterates this claim in Romans 16:20. "And the God of peace will soon crush Satan under your feet." This is a statement about *power*, not about clemency. To claim that Yeshua "is our peace" is to reiterate His claim that "all authority has been given to Me." "For He Himself is our peace, who made both *groups* [Jews and Gentiles] *into* one, and broke down the barrier of the dividing wall, by abolishing in His flesh the enmity, . . . and might reconcile them both in one body to God through the cross, by it having put to death the enmity."[63] If we translate the verse properly, we see that reconciliation removes the consequences of *disobedience*, and with these consequences removed, creation can return to its original design and purpose.

Ridderbos is generally correct when he says, "[T]he abrogation of this enmity through reconciliation is the same as being delivered from God's wrath, being acquitted of sin and guilt,"[64] but this applies the verse *only* to the despicable condition of men, and the verse clearly implies far more than that. "Peace on earth" is not simply a statement about forgiveness. It is about restoration.

---

[62] Ridderbos, *Paul*, p. 184.

[63] Ephesians 2:14-16 NASB. There are several translation assumptions based on replacement theology in the NASB rendition, not least of which is the deliberate addition of wording to make the verse read as if the enmity is "the Law of commandments contained in ordinances." These assumptions are unwarranted. See my work on this verse at http://skipmoen.com/tag/ephesians-215/

[64] Ridderbos, *Paul*, p. 185.

But this brings up another issue. Yeshua died. According to Paul, His blood on the cross brought peace. But look around you. Do you see God's peace spread across the globe? I certainly don't. Nevertheless, Paul says that this "peace" has been accomplished in Yeshua's death. The Greek is *eirenopoiesas*, the aorist, active participle of *eirenopoieo*, a combination of words meaning "to make peace." But the verb is a *completed action* (aorist). According to Paul, it's finished. Peace has been secured. How?

Paul can only have in mind the Hebrew idea of "first fruits." When the first of the harvest was offered to God, all the rest of the harvest was considered also sanctified. The first *represented* the whole. When Yeshua died, he overcame the final enemy, death itself. Peace was secured for the first fruit in His resurrection. As a result, all the rest, all those who follow Him, are guaranteed the same status, even though as yet we do not see it. Paul's view is eschatological. He looks over the horizon to see the *end* result resident in the present reality.

Now, we might argue that "peace with God" implies forgiveness. Yes, it does. But don't you see that the scope of the claim is so much bigger. The entire *cosmos* is involved in this event. It's not just about forgiving your sins. It's about *reordering the universe*. And it's been accomplished. We are just waiting to see it unfold.

We find the same idea in Yeshua's own words. *"The glory that you have given me I have given to*

114

them, that they may be one even as we are one."[65]
Certainly every Christian believer is familiar with
this Greek word – *doxa*. In days past, it was
incorporated into a ritual of Sunday worship. We
sang the *doxology*. But I wonder now if we ever
really understood the idea of glory. Yes, I am sure
we realized that God is glorious, that His splendor is
manifest in all that He does, that His reflection is
found in holiness, justice, mercy and compassion.
But how is it possible that Yeshua could say this
doxa has been given to us? Are we filled with
splendor? Are we reflections of holiness? Do we
manifest goodness, justice and mercy? It's hard for
me to see this in His followers. It's even more
difficult when I notice that the verb here (*dedoka*)
means that what Yeshua has given in the past has
continuing result in the present (the perfect tense in
Greek). The two verb tenses are the same. God
gave glory to Yeshua (an action in the past with
continuing results in the present). I can understand
that. Yeshua put aside divinity and became a man,
but the Father glorified Him – gave Him back what
He put aside – and He has that glory now and
forever – but you and me? How did Yeshua give us
glory and how does it still show up today?

Morris provides this explanation: "Just as His
[Yeshua's] true glory was to follow the path of
lowly service culminating in the cross, so for them
[the disciples] the true glory lay in the path of lowly
service wherever it might lead them."[66] Morris
amplifies this comment by adding that "the apostles
are right with God and therefore they are supremely

---

[65] John 17:22 ESV
[66] Leon Morris, *The Gospel According to John*, NICNT, p.
734.

115

significant. They have the true glory. They are walking in the way of God."[67] That all sounds so nice, but it doesn't seem to be true. Yeshua spoke these words just before His arrest. *None* of the apostles remained loyal to Him after that event. Is that "walking in the way of God"? Did they "take up the cross and follow"? It seems to me that Morris' comment is only accurate *after* the resurrection, but Yeshua says that He has already given them the equivalent glory of what He received. The perfect tense does not imply that they *will* receive it at some later point in time. It implies that the gift has already been given. Morris considers the "way of the cross" to be the "way of true glory." We might agree, but how can this be true of the apostles when Yeshua makes this statement? Maybe we just don't understand what "glory" means.

One thing is certain. Yeshua wasn't speaking Greek when He uttered these words. So examining the meaning of *doxa* is not going to help much. *Doxa* is used as the translation of twenty-five different Hebrew words in the LXX. But primarily it is associated with the Hebrew *kavod*. Rooted in the language of the land, *kavod* is about what is heavy, what has weight – and therefore has importance and significance. But since YHWH is invisible, *kavod* is used as a description of His *manifestation*. He *reveals* Himself as glorious. We find this sense of the word in the description of the *Shekhinah* falling on the Tabernacle, the vision of Ezekiel, the illumination of Moses' face and the transfiguration of Yeshua. *Kavod* is a description of

---

[67] *Ibid.*, p. 734-735.

the revelation of God in His acts in creation and salvation. Above all, it speaks of God's *honor*, exhibited in His self-revelation.

What does this mean to us for understanding Yeshua's statement? "The manifestation, self-revelation and honor you have given me, I have given to them." Has Yeshua passed to us the manifestation of YHWH? Have we become the vehicles of His honor? If we think of "glory" as a kind of possession, as a *state* of being that is somehow attached to us in the way that we acquire a gift when it becomes our property, then I am afraid we will misinterpret Yeshua's declaration. We will think of "glory" from a Greek paradigm, as though receiving glory is an expression of a quality that is now ours. "Glory" becomes an adjective in much the same way that "saved" becomes an adjective.

But if we think in Hebrew, then we notice the *kavod* is not something we possess. It is an act that we participate in. We *become* the manifestation. We *become* the honor and the revelation. We don't *have it*. We *are* what it is as it is displayed *through us*. Glory is a description of Yeshua *as He fulfills the purposes of the Father* because in that process He manifests the truth of YHWH. It is the same for us. Yeshua gives us the means and the opportunity to become the process of God's self-revelation. We are glory, the glory of the Father, precisely as Yeshua was the glory of the Father, *when we manifest the Father* in our actions.

This understanding of *doxa* (*kavod*) allows us to fully examine the conversation between Yeshua and

Pilate, a conversation that is critically important for the interpretation of the cross event.

Pilate therefore said to Him, "So You are a king?" Jesus answered, "You say correctly that I am a king. For this I have been born, and for this I have come into the world, to bear witness to the truth. Every one who is of the truth hears My voice."[68]

Yeshua's conversation with Pilate is about being a *king*, not about being a savior! Too often we think that the statement, "For this I have been born, and for this I have come into the world" is about saving us from sin. We have read this declaration as if Yeshua's focus was about atonement, substitutionary sacrifice and forgiveness. But now we must read this verse for what it *says*, not what we wanted it to say. And what it says is that Yeshua came to be king. He came to *rule*! He came to bear witness to the truth that *He is sovereign*. His kingdom does not originate on this earth. His power and authority come from above. And everyone who hears the message of His reign hears the truth of YHWH's purpose from the beginning.

If there were ever an opportunity for Yeshua to set the record straight, Pilate provided that opportunity. Facing certain death, Yeshua has no reason to disguise His real purpose. He doesn't falter. He speaks it plainly. His death is the means by which He will permanently establish the Kingdom of God on earth – *His kingdom* on earth! " . . . and you will see the Son of Man sitting at the right hand of

---

[68] John 18:37 NASB

power" (Mark 14:62). Can there be any doubt? The certainty of the cross is not the certainty of *our* forgiveness. It is the certainty that Yeshua is Lord over death, that His kingdom will never fade because this King lives forever.

How could we have missed it? He came to *die* because His death defeats the one enemy that *no earthly king can ever overcome.* How could we not see that the cross is about *death and life*? Those who follow Him to the cross, citizens of His kingdom, share in the victory won there. They have been given the power to live forever.

Yeshua's analogy of the serpent in the wilderness points us toward power. His use of prophetic imagery points us toward authority. His declaration before Pilate seems to be clear. His announcement before the Ascension is remarkably straightforward ("All authority has been given to Me"). In the process of demonstrating His place as the eternal King, forgiveness is also accomplished, but now that we read what the text actually says, we must conclude that our preoccupation with forgiveness is just a bit too self-centered. The grand plan of YHWH for the reunion of the Kingdom on earth as it is in heaven is just a bit bigger than our preoccupation with our sins.

One more passage underscores this change in perspective.

And the inscription of the charge against Him read, "THE KING OF THE JEWS."[69]

---

[69] Mark 15:26 NASB

The conversation between Yeshua and Pilate is about being king. The charge against Yeshua is about being king. The crime is sedition, incitement to rebel against a king. The crowds that want Him crucified proclaim Caesar as king. The cross is the symbol of the power of a king. What could be more obvious!

There's not a hint about an altar or a Temple or a Levitical sacrifice or a spotless offering. Everything points to *king*. Even death. The power to kill is the ultimate power of this world's kingdoms. When Yeshua says that if His kingdom found its origin in this world ("is not of this world") then His servants would fight, he implies that the means of maintaining power used by kingdoms of this world will not be the means by which His kingdom is maintained. Even in this, the topic is *kingdom*, not forgiveness. It takes interpretative additions and explanations to view these texts in the context of sin sacrifice. Of course, that doesn't mean that they *cannot* be viewed this way. It only means that it isn't obvious. What's obvious is that this is about kings, kingdoms and power. If it is also about forgiveness, then forgiveness is hidden in plain sight.

But this is a problem. Why? Because we have reversed the plain meaning of the text. For us, *forgiveness is what's obvious*. Therefore, we think that what's hidden is the topic of kings and kingdoms. We have Christian blinders on, and they prevent us from reading the text *as it is*. We read it according to our preconceived idea that Jesus died on the cross for the forgiveness of sin. Since it seems quite unlikely that anyone who observed this event would have drawn that conclusion, we must look to the authors of the New Testament to tell us how this event was interpreted after it occurred. First we notice that while many authors tell us that Yeshua's death atones for sin, none say that this death is the death *on the cross*.[70] We merely *assume* that they are speaking about the death on the cross because we don't see any other sacrificial death. Except, of course, that difficult verse, Revelation 13:8.

It's only one verse, you say. One verse against a mountain of doctrine. But what do you do with "For which is easier, to say, "Your sins are forgiven,' or to say, 'Rise, and walk'?" (Matthew 9:5) or the other incidents of forgiveness during Yeshua's earthly ministry? If Yeshua can forgive sins *before* the crucifixion, then how can atonement occur only *after* the crucifixion? Are we prepared to say that forgiveness grated by Yeshua prior to the crucifixion was based on some others means? What other means? And if it is based on the same means as you and I are forgiven, then is His declaration to the lame man merely proleptic? Does that man have to wait until *after* the crucifixion until he is "truly" forgiven?

But if forgiveness occurs in the heavenly Temple at the heavenly altar prior to the foundation of the world, then Yeshua forgives this lame man in precisely the same way that He forgives you and me

---

[70] There are a few verses that *appear* to connect forgiveness with the cross event. We will examine them in due order below.

– and everyone else who has ever lived. And then the cross must be about something else.

Christian theologians often point to the "cry of dereliction" as proof that Sin (with a capital S) was imputed to Yeshua *on the cross*. They cite this verse in Matthew.

And about the ninth hour Jesus cried out with a loud voice, saying, "Eli, Eli lama Sabachthani?" that is, "My God, My God, why hast Thou forsaken Me?"[71]

Christians often claim that at this moment God the Father abandoned the Son because "God cannot look upon sin." Jesus goes to the cross to act as our substitutionary sacrifice. He takes on the Sin of the world. God leaves Him at that terrible moment. Therefore, He cries out as He becomes Sin for us.

But if our prior analysis is correct, then this "cry" cannot be about the imputation of Sin. We need to address the typical Christian view about sin and death on the cross. Morris captures the point:

"We should not forget that these are the only words from the cross recorded by the first two evangelists. They must have selected them for a purpose. As they stand the words can scarcely be taken as anything other than a declaration that in the manner of His death Jesus was cut off from the Father."[72]

---

[71] Matthew 27:46 NASB
[72] Leon Morris, *The Cross in the New Testament*, p. 45.

But Morris' position ignores the *Jewish* context of this recital. Why should we take the words as a declaration of abandonment? We only read them in this fashion if we exclude the common practice among Jews in the first century of citing a psalm, a whole psalm, by referring to its opening verse. That's the way the books of the Pentateuch are named. Not Genesis, Exodus, Leviticus but *Bere'shiyt, Shemot, Va-yikra,* the words that open those books. There were *no* chapters, verse numbers or Greek names. If you wanted to remind someone of a book or a psalm, you had to give him someplace to start; and Psalm 22 is a psalm of vindication, not abandonment.

Furthermore, Morris admits that claiming the Father abandons the Son at this moment causes all kinds of problems for doctrines like the Trinity, for claims about the divine person of the Christ and for understanding how God could be *excluded* from this event. We might add that if David can legitimately say that God is present in Sheol, why do we think He can't be present here? Peter Green claims that "the cry of dereliction shows that the price of sin has been paid in full."[73] But if the Lamb is slain *before the foundation of the world,* then how can this cry be about paying for sin? Are we to ignore the statements of John, the author of Hebrews and of Peter because we have a theological paradigm that claims Jesus dealt with Sin on the cross?

What makes more sense – that the Father walked away from the Son in the moment He took on our sin, or that Yeshua was pointing all His detractors to

---

[73] Peter Green, *Studies in the Cross,* p. 81.

a psalm so that they would recognize His vindication? What would the Jewish audience at the cross have understood?

Chapter Four

Problems with Paul (and others)

We have argued that the cross event is about
restoration of the Kingdom through the defeat of
death. We have argued that the restoration removes
the last stronghold of the enemy's defilement of
creation. We have argued that while forgiveness is
a major concern of the biblical record, the
crucifixion does not fit any of the earthly patterns
for acceptable sacrifices for sin. We have argued
that biblical texts support the idea that atonement
was accomplished in the heavenly Temple before
the foundation of the world. We have argued that
this fact sets aside any separation of law and grace,
and that grace has always been the vehicle of
salvation. We have argued that Yeshua Himself
points to issues of power, authority and kingdom
when He provides clues about the meaning of the
cross – and finally, we have argued that no Jew in
the first century would have mistaken the cross as a
place of forgiveness.

But what do we do with Paul (and a few others)?
Doesn't Paul say over and over that the cross is
central to salvation? Doesn't Paul portray the cross
as the place of forgiveness? Does Paul have a
completely different view than his first-century
Jewish contemporaries, including Yeshua?
Christian apologists claim that he does. They claim
that Paul "converted" to a new religion called
Christianity, and that he abandoned the place of
Torah, the system of Levitical sacrifice and the
necessity of the "Law." They claim that Paul is

essentially in line with later Christian development of forgiveness of sin through the crucifixion. If this is true, then Paul is the real source of Christian thinking. After all, we have shown rather conclusively that Yeshua's thinking about the cross does not involve forgiveness of sin; but if Paul argues that it does, then we have uncovered a major schism in Scripture.

Therefore, it is incumbent upon us to re-examine the Pauline verses that Christian apologists use to support the claim that Jesus died on the cross for the forgiveness of sin. That's precisely what we will do, one verse at a time.

The Texts

knowing that Christ, having been raised from the dead, is never to die again; death no longer is master over Him. Romans 6:9 NASB

We have investigated Yeshua's claim about the meaning of the cross, but we haven't looked deeply into Paul's declarations. We can start with this one. But before we do, we need to make something clear. The cross is at the very heart of the gospel. The cross represents an action of YHWH that changes the world. It is possible to draw a connection between what happened on the cross and the forgiveness God offers. But that doesn't mean that the cross is *directly about forgiveness.* Let's look deeper.

Notice the emphasis of Paul's remark. Yeshua's death and resurrection are directly related to the *power of death.* Death no longer "is master." The

Greek is *ouketi kyrieuei*. This is a very strong statement. First, it employs the combination of *ou* (*ouk*) and *eti*, meaning "it is not ever any longer the case." In other words, there will never again be a time when this occurs. What is it that will never ever occur again? The rule of death! The dominion of the grave. Here Paul uses the word *kyrieuei* (from *kyrieuo* – to rule). You might recognize one of the cognates, *kyrios*, the title used often in the New Testament for Yeshua as "Ruler" or "Lord." Paul's point is obvious. The death and resurrection of Yeshua *conquers death*. It is determined that every man will die once, and Yeshua did die once. Therefore, He will never die again; and since He nevertheless lives, He demonstrates that God has power over even death. In this way we know that forgiveness is complete, for death is the result of sin. Now the Son has guaranteed that death no longer reigns supreme over men. The final stranglehold on men has been removed. As a result of this public demonstration, we now are assured that death's dominion over men is finished. If it could not hold Yeshua, it also cannot hold all those who have been sanctified in Yeshua.

What is the meaning of the cross? The cross is the first century cultural symbol of the power of death. No other symbol carried such a clear and unmistakable message. The cross was death itself; and the paramount symbol of the hideous rule death has over men. Today we might substitute another symbol. Perhaps an atomic mushroom cloud or a gas chamber or the Swastika. In the first century in Israel, the cross represented this terrible power in the hands of a pagan empire; and YHWH used this vehicle to bring about a sign of eternal, never-to-die-again, life. What is the meaning of the cross? It is the sign that *death is done! Fear is finished.* The long wait before the dawn is over.

In Him we have redemption through His blood, the forgiveness of our trespasses, according to the riches of His grace. Ephesians 1:7 NASB

When did we receive redemption through the blood of Yeshua? There are several perfectly correct answers. The first answer is entirely personal. *You* were personally redeemed when you experienced the joy of recognizing that your sins were forgiven. That timing will be slightly different for every repentant human being who came to the Lord. The second answer is general. God provided the means for your experience of forgiveness through the blood of Yeshua at a time He designated, regardless of your awareness of that offer. Your personal participation in His offer of grace depends on a *prior arrangement.* Obvious, and true. Now the question becomes, "When did God make this arrangement?" Most Christians answer this second question according to the teaching of the Church. They say that the offer of forgiveness was arranged at the time of the death of Yeshua on the cross. But just for the moment, let's consider this answer. Was the offer of grace made available at the moment Yeshua died? If that's true, then what is the purpose of the resurrection? Why do we need a resurrected Christ if His mission was accomplished at death? Would you revise your answer slightly and suggest that the *resurrection* was the seal of the atonement? But if that's true, then why does the Church teach that our sins were forgiven *on the cross*? And then there's the further complication.

If God's arrangement for the offer of forgiveness occurs on the cross, then what about all those devoted followers of YHWH who lived before the crucifixion? How were their sins forgiven? Retroactively? Or were their sins somehow held in heavenly limbo until the crucifixion? The standard replacement theology answer is that prior to the cross salvation was thought to be an effort of "works." After the cross, we now realize that it is based on grace. But this standard answer is not only woefully misconstrued on biblical grounds, it also misrepresents the lives and theology of devoted followers of YHWH from Abraham to John the Baptist. They all knew it was grace. It was always grace. They weren't waiting for the *cross* to find forgiveness because they already experienced forgiveness directly from God. In addition to all this confusion, we have the prophets – prophets who reveal *from God* that what is required is to love mercy, do justice and follow Torah.[74] No mention of waiting for the Messiah to forgive you. Strange, don't you think, especially if forgiveness is *the single greatest issue Man will ever face*!

Does this verse from Paul's letter teach us that forgiveness occurs on the cross? I don't see how it can unless we have already concluded that this is what it says, in spite of the fact that the cross isn't mentioned. What is says is that we are forgiven through the blood of Yeshua according to God's grace; but, it says *nothing* about how or when that provision was made. For that we have to look somewhere else. As we will see, nearly *all* of Paul's declarations about redemption and atonement

---

[74] Cf. Micah 6:8

have the same ambiguity. The substance is clear. The timing isn't.

Paul, an apostle of Christ Jesus by the will of God, according to the promise of life in Christ Jesus, 2 Timothy 1:1 NASB

Paul's *second* letter opening contains some changes. From his first letter to Timothy. They are worth noting. First we see that Paul is still an apostle but now this is by the *will* of God, not by God's command (as in 1 Timothy 1:1). What's the difference? Actually, not much. The Greek *thelema* is distinguished from *boulomai* by the fact that this verb describes what is not only intended or desired, but what is *also completed*. When *thelema* is used of God, it means that God's intention is brought to execution. Man may intend, but not complete. God intends *and completes*. He finishes what He starts. So when Paul uses the Greek *thelema* of God's will, he does not mean that God simply desired it. He means that God made it happen – and that is essentially the equivalent of a commandment. From Paul's perspective, it is what God demands. From God's perspective, it is what He does.

In the first letter, Paul notes that the commandment that causes him to be an apostle is related to the Messiah who is our hope. Here Paul sees that hope as the promise of life. There seem to be two striking elements in this change. The first is the *absence* of any suggestion about forgiveness from sin. We might have wondered about this with Paul's first opening because there he speaks of God as savior; but now, when he is given a second opportunity to mention forgiveness from sin, he

130

doesn't. Instead, he points us toward the promise of life. What is that promise?

If we remember those passages connecting Yeshua to the cross, we could draw the conclusion that the promise of life is, in fact, the guarantee that death has been overcome and is no longer the end of the story. We could go on to recognize that if the Messiah is the first fruit of those who follow Him, He guarantees the sanctification of the followers so that they too participate in this life without end. We could remember all of the Messiah's comments about the kingdom at hand and the power and authority that He has been given after the resurrection. We could reach back to the Garden and realize that the promise of life began there with the tree of life, now realized in the work of the Messiah. We could think of all of this as part of the Jewish consciousness of the living God; and we might draw the conclusion that the role of the embodied Messiah had something to do with life and death, not forgiveness from sin.

Then we would have to reflect on Paul's use of *kata* (according to). You remember that word. It is part of the phrase in 1 Timothy 1:1 ("according to the commandment of God our savior"). Paul uses *kata* in this opening verse too; but whereas before it was "according to the commandment," now it is "according to the promise." Interesting. Are we supposed to recognize that the commandment *is* the promise?

I charge you in the presence of God, who gives life to all things, and of Christ Jesus, who testified the good confession before Pontius Pilate; 1 Timothy 6:13 NASB

Paul gives orders to Timothy. Those orders still govern us because we are volunteers committed to the same way of life Paul expressed. Paul's directions to Timothy are Paul's directions to all Gentiles who choose the Way. Of course, we *choose* to follow them. We are not compelled; but once we accept this Way, the orders apply. Agreed?

The orders Paul gives are in the next verse, but without the context of this verse, they might easily be misunderstood. So let's start here with the context. Notice that even if Paul didn't believe he was writing sacred script, he clearly understood that what he was telling Timothy came with the authority of YHWH. We accept these orders on the basis of their divine origin, not simply because Paul gives them. Notice also that Paul clearly describes this origin in terms of *life*, not death. YHWH is the God who gives *life* to all things. Are you alive? Then you live because of God's *gift*. You don't live on your own merit or because of your own efforts. Life is God's *gift* to you; and since it is His gift, you are obligated to Him. We often think of a gift as something that comes without any strings attached, but this is not quite the case here. While the gift of life was not given in order that you must serve Him – as all the other ancient Near-Eastern religions believed – this gift does come with a condition. That condition is to be found worthy of the gift. It is not a gift given so that you become God's slave; but it does carry responsibility. You are expected to warrant the offer.

As if this were not enough, Paul employs a second source of authority, namely, the *good confession* of Yeshua before Pilate. Now we need to pay very close attention. We have the tendency to think that this good confession is the same as our confessions of trust in "Jesus" for salvation; but this is not what Yeshua revealed before Pilate. And, by the way, if the good confession were nothing more than the theology of salvation, why would it be the basis for *orders*? Why would Pilate care anything for orders associated with a claim to forgive sin? Go back to the dialogue between Yeshua and Pilate and you will see why this good confession is the basis of authority. Yeshua does not reveal His divinity or His role in atonement. He reveals Himself as *King*! That's why these orders carry weight. They come from the *King of the Universe!*

What is the "good confession"? The Greek is *kalen homologian* – literally "saying the same good thing." But this begs the question, "The same as what?" Here we realize that Paul must have heard this "good confession" from someone else. He wasn't there when it happened. In fact, no one except Yeshua and Pilate knew of this confession. So the content of the confession came by way of revelation, either from Yeshua Himself or from another divine source; and the content of the confession must align with the rest of Yeshua's teaching if it is to qualify as "good." I can think of only one theme that is echoed in the conversation with Pilate. It is this: "The kingdom of heaven is at hand." The reason we must follow Paul's orders is that God is life and Yeshua is King. The reason that this is *homologian* is that these two statements reiterate the overall purpose of God. We owe Him our lives and we owe Him our obedience. The "good confession" is that Yeshua is Lord of life. It's not about forgiveness of sins. It's about the one who *rules*.

For He rescued us from the domain of darkness, and transferred us to the kingdom of His beloved Son, in whom we have redemption, the forgiveness of sins. Colossians 1:13-14 NASB

This Pauline statement is often used to prove that Yeshua's death on the cross accomplished the atonement of our sins. The argument is that Paul clearly connects redemption with the forgiveness of sins, and therefore, with the cross. But that exegesis is based on theological assumptions about atonement, not on this text. If we read the text carefully, paying attention to the pronouns, we discover that Paul tells us that God the Father, the one and only God, is responsible for our deliverance and citizenship in the Kingdom. *He* rescued us. *He* transferred us.

There are some other noteworthy facts in these verses. First, we see that Paul recognizes that the Kingdom is the Kingdom of the Son. This fits nicely with Yeshua's claim before Pilate (it's all about kings and kingdoms). Secondly, we see that Paul thinks of YHWH as the one who initiated these actions. This fits the Hebraic construction found in *yasad* and *kun*. Thirdly, there is a significant and critical role for the Son to play in these events. Redemption comes *through* the Son. It is initiated by the Father but obtained through the Son. Finally, we note that Paul uses "forgiveness of sins" as the equivalent of "redemption." Are we to conclude that these statements mean Yeshua died on the cross for our redemption? That claim extends the verses beyond their actual words.

Notice that these verses do not say *when* or *how* redemption became available. These verses can be equally true of redemption obtained by the sacrifice in the heavenly Temple before the foundation of the world (as John tells us in Revelation). All these verses say is that the Father initiated the events and the Son carried them out; but there is no necessity to apply these to the cross. All these verses say is that Yeshua accomplished the means of redemption, but there is no indication that it took place *on the cross*. In fact, if we see that the background to Paul's claim is an awareness of *kingdom* issues, then we should pay much more attention to the *kingdom* claims of Yeshua before Pilate. Furthermore, it is difficult to imagine that forgiveness of sins was not available before the crucifixion, especially since Yeshua offers forgiveness prior to His death.

What we have is a conundrum of theological importance. Christianity nearly universally teaches that atonement occurs on the cross; but this requires us to sidestep Yeshua's own declarations of forgiveness prior to crucifixion, and it requires us to modify statements by John and Peter and the author of Hebrews. Furthermore, it significantly alters the theme that it is the Father who brings about redemption *because* of the actions of the Son – not the Son who redeems on His own. The path of Jewish practice in the first century doesn't have these difficulties, not because it rejects Yeshua's claims (in fact, many Jews did not reject his claims) but because atonement was always initiated by

YHWH through the Levitical sacrifices on the altar. From a Jewish perspective, Yeshua does not replace the goal, which is the removal of defilement and subsequent restoration of fellowship with God. He only replaces the means by which it is accomplished. Paul says nothing more than this.

having cancelled out the certificate of debt consisting of decrees against us and which was hostile to us; and He has taken it out of the way, having nailed it to the cross. Colossians 2:14 NASB

The Greek texts shows us that what was nailed to the cross was the *cheirographon*, the Greek word for a certificate of debt, that is, an IOU. There is no justification for claiming that the law behind the certificate was removed. Just because my traffic ticket is voided does not mean that the law establishing the case for the ticket is void. In biblical terms, Torah applies. The *penalty* produced by Torah disobedience does not apply. Those who read this verse in the NIV will be led astray by the NIV's deliberate translation supporting replacement theology; but this theological manipulation of the text does not hold up when we examine the Greek. Paul never suggests that the Law itself is removed; only that the penalty (the IOU) is removed, and that penalty is *death*! Forgiveness of sins is *not* a penalty. It is a benefit. Therefore, this Pauline statement connects the cross to the *penalty*, not the benefit. We have to *add* the idea that forgiveness occurred on the cross. Paul didn't say that.

Exegetes who argue that this verse supports the claim that Jesus died on the cross for the forgiveness of sin point to the pronoun "it" ("having nailed it") claiming that "it" refers to "sin." But this is also unwarranted. "It" is the certificate of debt. The Greek text makes this abundantly clear. What did the certificate of debt imply? What is the penalty for disobedience? Death! When Yeshua nailed the certificate to the cross, He removed the *penalty*! The penalty is not our sins. It is death. The cross is the place of death, both literally and figuratively. On it God reversed the direction of the universe. God overcame death by death – the death of His blameless Son who knew no certificate of debt.

Try reading the verse with this in mind. The certificate of debt is the direct result of disobedience. In fact, possessing a *cheirographon* implies the existence of a *valid* standard – a law. There can be no debt if there is no standard of payment. How did the certificate arise? Paul tells us that it came into existence because of decrees leveled against us. That is exactly what happens when we disobey the law. We create a situation where we *owe*. We owe because the law applies and in its application it creates the need for payment. Yeshua *removes the payment required* by substituting Himself. But this does *not* imply that the cross is the place of substitution. What Paul says about the cross in this verse is that it is the place of cancellation of the *penalty*. Paul distinguishes the *payment* from the *penalty*. Atonement is the means of forgiveness. Removing the penalty of death is the sign of victory over defilement. In other words, this is a two-step process, with both steps intimately connected. First atonement is accomplished, clearing the way for the defilement to be eliminated. Yeshua's sacrifice provides the means by which God re-establishes relationship. This applies in Genesis 3:21, just as much as it applies today; but secondly, the defilement created by death itself must be overcome. The creation must be cleansed. This is accomplished by the resurrection from the dead of one who carried no penalty. Death is defeated in an *unjustified* death. The nails are the instruments of life.

Perhaps we have been led astray by 1800 years of self-justifying theology. Perhaps it's time to read Paul as a Jew.

But when the fullness of the time came, God sent forth His Son, born of a woman, born under the Law, so that He might redeem those who were under the Law, that we might receive adoption as sons. Galatians 4:4-5 NASB

Once again we confront a Pauline connection between "redeem" and references to the earthly ministry of Yeshua. The Greek verb for "redeem" is *exagorazo*. It literally means, "to purchase out of." The root of the verb, *agorazo*, comes from the noun, *agora*, which in turn means "the marketplace." So this verb in Galatians recalls the imagery of going to the market to buy something once owned by the purchaser. According to the usage in Paul, Yeshua bought us back. The action is dynamic, not static. It is the *process* of the repurchase that matters.

But this begs a question that is almost never asked. What did Yeshua buy us back from? Who was the present owner when He came to repurchase us? Don't think that Paul says we were *owned* by the Law! It isn't the Law that was our slave master. Paul describes us as "under the Law," not "owned by the Law." What's the difference? The Law (Torah) established God's instructions for life and the punishment for disobedience. Because we are under its umbrella, we are subject to its requirements and consequences. Being under the Torah, i.e., being subjected to its stipulations, we find that our disobedience demands our death. But it is *death* that owns us, not the Torah. We are held captive by death due to our failure to keep Torah. We don't need to be redeemed from the Law; we need to be redeemed from the result of breaking the Law! If we had kept Torah, there would be no need to be redeemed from Torah for keeping it guarantees life. Our problem is not the standard. It is the consequence of not keeping the standard.

Yeshua comes to *buy us back from the death sentence* that hangs over each of us. This fits perfectly with the Hebrew idea of redemption. In Hebrew thought, redemption (deliverance, salvation, return) makes no sense unless there is an immediate threat to life itself. So if you ask a Jew today, "Are you saved?" he will probably respond, "From what?" No threat – no need for redemption. For Paul this means that I only understand *exagorazo* in terms of *thanatos* (death). Just as Yeshua was bought back from the grave, so He buys me back from the inevitable and justified termination of my life. To be redeemed is to be brought back to *life*! And Paul notes that only those who have been brought back to life may be adopted as sons.

Why was Yeshua born? Why did He come into the world at the *kairos* moment? So that He might live under the same standard that we do (Torah) and by perfectly fulfilling it, *but dying anyway*, He might substitute His death for yours and mine and bring us back to life. In this passage, does Paul say that Yeshua will redeem us from *sin*? That's how we would usually read this statement, but notice that it doesn't say that. In fact, *sin* isn't the issue. It's the *consequence of sin* that's the issue. God has provided many ways of dealing with sin, but until there is a way of dealing with the consequences, forgiveness doesn't accomplish much (is this too bold to say?). If you were Paul, and you wanted to communicate a compelling message to a pagan audience, would you tell them that they could be forgiven of their *sins* or would you tell them that there was an answer to the specter of *death*?

For I delivered to you as of first importance what I also received, that Christ died for our sins according to the Scriptures, and that He was buried, and that He was raised on the third day, according to the Scriptures, . . . 1 Corinthians 15:3-4 NASB

In what sense did Yeshua HaMashiach die for us? Paul says *hyper hamartion*. We translate "for our sins" since the noun is a plural genitive. But what does *hyper* mean? Riesenfeld has an interesting comment. "Paul develops the saving significance of Christ's death with the help of typology in Gal. 3:13 and 2 Cor. 5:21. Jesus in his death vicariously takes the curse for us, and thus secures our liberation from the law. In this context *hypér* has the sense of

'in our favor' but also 'in our place or stead.'"[75]
Did you notice Riesenfeld's assumption that the
curse is the *law*? And this is in the most prestigious
theological dictionary of the New Testament.
Accordingly, Paul uses *hyper* in the sense of "in our
favor" or "in our place." This is substitutionary
atonement in Christian terms. It is the innocent
Lamb slain instead of the sinner.

But wait a minute! Paul certainly knows that the
Passover Lamb was not slain as a sin sacrifice. It
was slain so that the angel of death would pass over.
Paul also certainly knows that the sin sacrifice of
Yom Kippur is not slain, but rather sent into the
desert outside the camp. So Paul can't be referring
to Passover as a symbol of sin sacrifice, nor can he
be referring to the atonement offered at Yom
Kippur. All he says is that Yeshua HaMashiach
died for our sins *kata graphas* (according to the
Scriptures). According to what Scriptures? What
Scripture teaches us that Yeshua had to die to
deliver us from sin? That must be the Servant Song
of Isaiah 53, especially verses 5 and 6.

We examined the Isaiah passage in relation to the
cross (see TW March 18-19, 2013). Peter refers to
the same Servant Song as an example of righteous
suffering, adding "the cross" to the Isaiah text; but
Paul doesn't gloss Isaiah. He merely *breaks* the
Servant Song from the next claim about death and
resurrection. In other words, Paul gives us two
important related, but not inseparable, facts.

---

[75] Kittel, G., Friedrich, G., & Bromiley, G. W. (1985).
Abridged *Theological Dictionary of the New Testament* (p.
1228). Grand Rapids, MI: W.B. Eerdmans.

Yeshua died for our sins (referring to Isaiah) *and* Yeshua was buried and rose again (referring most likely to Jonah, perhaps Hosea 6:2 and Psalm 16:10). Both claims are *kata graphas*. Why would Paul separate them as two independent clauses? Why not lump both claims under one "according to Scripture" endorsement? Could it be that Paul recognized a temporal/theological distinction between dying for sins and death-resurrection? We don't know for sure, but it is curious. Paul clearly saw *some* reason for separating the claims. Perhaps he and John ("before the foundation") aren't so far apart after all.

Let's suppose for the sake of argument that the sacrifice of Yeshua actually took place on the heavenly altar in the heavenly Temple before the foundation of the world (as Scripture says). Let's suppose that those verses in Revelation, 1 Peter and Hebrews actually mean what they say and that, as a result, the atoning removal of defilement that prevents being in the presence of YHWH was anticipated and made available before sin showed up on this planet. If this is true, then in what sense is it correct to say that Yeshua "died on the cross for our sins." It is possible to read this phrase in two different ways. The first is the way that Christians usually read this verse. Jesus died on the cross *because* of our sins. Christians usually think of His death in these terms. Because we sinned, atonement was needed and that atonement was accomplished on the cross. In other words, the cross event occurred in order to make provision for the sins we committed. The cross is the direct result of the need for forgiveness. In this reading, the preposition *hyper* expresses *causality*.

But other writings of Paul suggest a different reading. *Hyper* can also express *consequence*. Then the phrase means, "as a result of the consequences of our disobedience, Yeshua died on the cross." In other words, the consequence of sin is death and as a result of our sins, Yeshua died, not to cover over the sins but to remove the consequences. He died in order that *death might be erased from the creation*, that is, that the defilement produced by disobedience and epitomized in death might be wiped away. This reading upholds Paul's assertion that the "law" is good and holy, while suggesting that it is *death* that is conquered on the cross. In this reading, the phrase "for our sins" should be read as "in order to erase the consequences of our sins." It is appropriate Hebrew thought to use "for our sins" as shorthand for "for the curse resulting from our sins" because "sin" and "consequences of disobedience" can be understood as equivalent.

Why do we care about this Hebraic shorthand? Does it really matter? If we read the verse as most Christian theologians, we must *supply* the background that the cross is a means of atonement. But if the verse can also mean that the cross deals with the resulting *consequences* of sin and is not necessarily a place of atonement, then we are jolted into the awareness that interpretation of the verse depends on a paradigm. In other words, the *paradigm* determines the meaning, not the words themselves. And that leads us to ask, "Where did we get the paradigm? Where did the idea that the cross is the place of atonement come from if it didn't come from the verse itself?" That leads us to ask, "If Paul is a Jewish rabbi, would he have thought of the cross as a place of atonement?" And suddenly we realize that this "sacred cow" is precariously standing on one leg.

He disarmed the rulers and authorities and put them to open shame, by triumphing over them in him. Colossians 2:15 ESV

Despite the popular claim that "Jesus" died on the cross for the forgiveness of sin, we find that the biblical texts say something else. They say that forgiveness (atonement) has been available since before the foundation of the world although its full extent and deeper meaning has been progressively revealed to us over time. We also found that the cross is not a place of sin sacrifice, but rather the manifestation of God's redemptive work in the defeat of the consequences of sin, that is, the death of death. The cross demonstrates that God uses the tool of the enemy to overturn even the greatest threat of the enemy, and in so doing, establishes a kingdom like no other – an *eternal and imperishable presence of the Lord of life.*

Our investigation dealt with the mistake of reading the apparent future tense claims of New Testament passages as if they describe Greek static states rather than Hebrew dynamic processes. We didn't examine *all* the passages but we saw enough to recognize that the claims that such-and-such *will* happen does not imply that it is not already present in its nascent form. This is particularly important in order to understand that the Bible is *one* book, not two testaments.

Finally we noticed that Yeshua Himself doesn't point to the cross as a place of atonement. Instead, He directs us to Moses' use of the *nes* as a symbol of God's triumph over the pagan threat of death, and He clearly states that His mission was to establish His rightful place as King in the eternal Kingdom. Since one of the key principles of biblical exegesis is that the Bible interprets the Bible (i.e., we look at other scriptures in order to understand a particular text), Yeshua's claims have enormous weight in settling the question about the cross.

Perhaps Paul's Jewish rabbinic perspective has been lost in our penchant to read into Paul what later Christian theology proposed. This verse in Colossians is a prime example. From an evangelical theological point of view, we are apt to claim that this verse is about Jesus' triumph over sin. As my faithful antagonist says, "It looks like both atonement and the defeat of the demonic powers were accomplished by the cross." But is this what the verse says? What is the object of the Greek verb *thriambeuo* (translated "to triumph over")? Does this verse claim that Yeshua's victory is over *sin*?

Let's consider the opening verb ("having disarmed the powers"). *Apekdyomai* comes from two Greek words literally meaning "to strip away from." According to this passage (verses 13-15), Yeshua stripped away (disarmed) the power of rulers and authorities in a *publicly observable manner*. They were put to shame, and in a Hebrew world, that means public shame, something that can be seen. This is not about invisible demonic forces. How would anyone know that they have been shamed? Where am I to look to see their crestfallen countenances? If rulers and authorities have been *disarmed*, what was taken from them? Certainly not their *claims* or superiority! What was taken from them is the ultimate basis of their power, that is, the threat of death! If a man does not fear to die because he is assured that the King of glory has granted him eternal life, is there any ruler or authority on earth that can compel his obedience? When Yeshua removed the *consequence* of sin, he stripped every earthly power of its ultimate threat. The triumph is His victory over the one thing that holds all unredeemed men captive – not sin but death. This triumph is *public* because the resurrection is a real, historical fact.

It seems so obvious when we look at the text. There is no mention of the cross, no mention of forgiveness of sin, no mention of demonic powers. Ah, but you object. The NIV translates this verse as "triumphing over them by the cross." A quick review of the Nestle-Aland 27th edition of the Greek New Testament reveals *no such wording in the text or in any alternate fragment of the text*. In other words, those words "by the cross" have been added to the translation. The NIV makes a marginal note, "Or them in him," but the marginal note is the *correct* reading, not an alternate. The NIV has deliberately altered the text, not on the basis of a possible alternate translation, but on the basis of a theological bias for which there is *no textual justification*.

No wonder we think Jesus died on the cross for the forgiveness of sin. That's what Christian

146

theologians want us to think. What a mess! Of course, this raises an important question. If the text doesn't contain "the cross," why did the NIV translators feel it necessary to *add* these words?

So, why did Yeshua die on the cross? Paul does *not* say anything about atonement or forgiveness in this verse. He says that the supposed power of public rulers and authorities has been stripped away from them. And how do you suppose that happened?

The Rest of the Crowd

It seems clear that the Pauline texts can be read in support of our general thesis that the cross is about the defeat of death, not the forgiveness of sins. We have covered enough texts from a variety of Paul's writings to demonstrate that what Paul says is in concert with what any Jewish rabbi of the first century would have understood about atonement. But Paul isn't the only author who speaks about this subject, and Christian apologists have marshaled forces from both the Tanakh and the writings of the apostles to support their claim. Let's examine some of these additional texts to see if our argument still holds.

We will start with prophetic verses from the Tanakh.

" . . . for I will forgive their iniquity, and their sin I will remember no more." Jeremiah 31:34 NASB

This text from Jeremiah appears to claim that forgiveness is still in the future, that is, it has not already been offered at the time Jeremiah gave this prophecy. If that is the case, then our claim that atonement was accomplished "before the foundation of the world" must be incorrect. Let's see what Jeremiah really says.

When does God forgive? You might answer, "At the moment you repent?" That seems correct until we ask, "Did God forgive prior to the death of Yeshua?" Maybe what you meant to say is that now that the crucifixion has taken place, God forgives immediately upon repentance but prior to the cross, He forgave with an eye toward the future crucifixion. In other words, He forgave eschatologically, applying forgiveness in a kind of retroactive way after the future event of the cross. That interpretation allows Jeremiah's prophecy to be about the *future* cross event when "I will forgive their iniquity" would become a reality.

There's just a small problem. The Jeremiah declaration is about the time of the renewed covenant, a time when "they will all know Me, from the least of them to the greatest of them," when teaching is no longer needed because all men follow Torah from the heart. As far as I can tell, that time has not yet arrived. It will – someday – when the Messiah returns to establish His kingdom on earth. But until then this prophecy is about events that have not yet occurred. And that means that the declaration "I will forgive" has not occurred either. If Jeremiah's words are about the future coming "new" covenant kingdom, then his words about forgiveness must also be about the future coming forgiveness. That implies that we are *all* waiting to be forgiven, not for the cross but for the fullness of the kingdom to arrive on earth. You can't have it both ways. You can't insist that half the verse is about the coming covenant kingdom but the other half of the verse is about something that has already occurred on the cross.

What's even more difficult is that this Hebrew verb is in a Qal form. That means it is a kind of *present* tense. It is also an imperfect. That means it is a continuing action. When God speaks to Jeremiah, His forgiveness is already a reality (as the entire Tanakh affirms) but it is not yet finished. It will go on until *all* iniquity is forgotten. This statement is true today and it was true at the time Jeremiah declared it. Forgiveness is not postponed until the cross or until the return of the King. It is manifest now, but it will be even more apparent later. This verse does not imply that we are waiting for forgiveness. It implies that forgiveness is now an *incomplete* act that will finally be finished in the renewed covenant kingdom. Those who see this verse as if it implies God was *waiting* until the cross in order to forgive, simply misunderstand the Hebrew Qal imperfect.

Why do we care about *when*? We care because the Bible affirms that God has always forgiven, from Genesis to Revelation. The foundation for that forgiveness is the atonement provided by the obedience of the Son. Adam is forgiven on exactly the same basis as you and me. He is forgiven because of Yeshua's faithfulness. What this means is that there is *no* separation between the redemptive process of the Tanakh and the writings of the apostles. We all come on the same grounds and for the same reason. That's why we are children of Abraham.

149

God forgives – now! As soon as we repent (and if the stories in the gospels are true, sometimes even though we have not repented), God forgives. The action of forgiveness is possible throughout human history because atonement has already been accomplished *before the world was created.* If you don't believe this, then you had better settle in for a long haul, because God tells you in Jeremiah that it won't actually become reality until the return of the King.

It seems clear that a proper reading of the verb tenses in Jeremiah, and an appreciation for the Hebraic context of this claim, still support the idea that forgiveness and atonement occurred long before Yeshua went to the cross.

Perhaps a favorite verse in the Psalms gives credence to the popular Christian claim.

*Your eyes have seen my unformed substance; and in Your book were all written the days that were **ordained for me**, when as yet there was not one of them.* Psalm 139:16 NASB

This verse is often used as a proof text for the idea that God has foreordained the days of our lives, in fact, every day of the cosmos. In theological terms, such a doctrine implies a strong view of omniscience and predestination. That is to say, if this verse really proves that God has ordained every day from the beginning, and God is infallibly correct in His knowledge of each and every one of these days, then it follows (logically) that no day ever occurs which has not already been conceived and orchestrated by God.[76] As you can readily see, such a view, in spite of its antiquity in Christian thought, violates our usual perception of free will and moral choice. A great deal of theological gymnastics, worthy of Olympic gold, have gone into reconciling this idea with the ubiquitous experience of human choice, but that is not the subject of this short reflection.[77]

But does this verse justify the further claim that the day of Yeshua's crucifixion was destined from before the formation of the world in such a way that it was *impossible* for it to have occurred on any other day except that day in the first century, and in any other way except in precisely the way it occurred. The argument goes something like this: God planned *every day* as it actually occurs before the formation of the world. Therefore, God planned the death of Yeshua on the cross from before creation. Because God planned it, He foreordained that it would occur as it did. God's foreordination entails that whatever God plans will, in fact, be the case. Therefore, Yeshua's death on the cross *had to occur* exactly as it was planned. And this entails that Yeshua *had no choice* in this matter, since God foreordained it to occur.

---

[76] Objectors often wish to separate the idea of God's knowledge from the execution of that knowledge (cf. Augustine), but the nature of God prevents such a separation even if we humans see the separation in our lives. God's *infallible* knowing entails the actual *execution* of what He knows. Human beings don't have this connection because they are not infallible.

[77] If you really want to follow the complete articulation of this idea and my critique of its failure both logically and biblically, then order my book, *God, Time and the Limits of Omniscience*.

Please note this corollary. If Yeshua's death on the cross is the logical result of God's foreordination, then it follows that it was not possible for Yeshua to *choose* any other path and, logically, all those verses that suggest that this was a choice Yeshua made are, in fact, delusions on his behalf and fabrications on our behalf. In truth, He had no choice and neither do we.

Clearly something is amiss. Either the entire human race has been under a spellbinding false impression that we actually *choose* what we do or this idea of predestination is somehow flawed. Ubiquitous human experience shows that the latter is the case. Therefore, the use of Psalm 139:16 as a proof text for the *inevitability* of the cross isn't quite so comforting. Not only does reading the verse in this way open up a can of worms so big that we could catch whales, it also has *no impact whatsoever* on the theological meaning of the cross event. The verse offers only a poetic reflection of the author's view of God's sovereignty. It says nothing about the cross, and, as we have argued, it says nothing about the larger idea of foreordination. It just isn't clear that this poet expresses an eternal truth about God's sovereign control over every day. It is clear that the poet, at this moment, *feels* that his life is completely under God's control, but it is a long step from this poetic feeling to a doctrine that puts the responsibility of *every action* in God's lap instead of ours. In fact, a bit more reading of the same poet would show that he is completely comfortable with the opposing idea that *he is responsible for his own choices* and that his choices are *real*!

One further note. It's interesting that the NASB adds the prepositional phrase "for me" in "the days that were ordained *for me*." The Hebrew text reads only *yamim yutstsaru*, "the days that were formed." The verse uses the same verb found in the creation account, *yatsar*, "to form, to fashion." The addition of the prepositional phrase shifts the focus from God's *general* creative activity to the *specific* days of this individual. The text doesn't say that, even if it *might* imply it.

What have we learned from this little adventure? Perhaps Walter Kaiser's comment suffices:

> The facile linking of assorted Biblical texts because of what appears on a prima facie reading to be similar wording or subject matter (usually called the proof-text method) must be resisted since it fails to establish that all of the texts being grouped together do indeed share the same theological or factual content.[78]

We might also add that you'd better be prepared to live with the theology if you want to use a verse to prove your point.

Let's consider another attempt to justify the Christian claim from a reference in the Tanakh. This involves claims about forgiving Israel.

"So I will establish my covenant with you, and you will know that I am the Lord. **Then***, when I make*

---

[78] Walter Kaiser, *Toward an Exegetical Theology*, 1981, p. 134

153

atonement for you for all you have done, you will remember and be ashamed and never again open your mouth because of your humiliation, declares the Sovereign Lord." Ezekiel 16:62-63 NIV (emphasis added)

When did God forgive Israel? Perhaps a follow-up question makes the point. When did God forgive *you*? Through the prophet Ezekiel, YHWH gives us some insight into the answers. According to YHWH's statement, He will establish his covenant *after* He makes atonement. At least that's what you would think if you read the text in the NIV. This leads us to conclude that the covenant and the atonement are two separate events. The covenant comes first and the atonement comes later.

But what if I told you that the word "then" does *not* appear in the Hebrew text. Both the ESV and the NASB do not include this extra temporal condition. The Hebrew text reads *kelimatek bekapperilak* ("your shame when I atone"). There is no *extra temporal condition.* The NIV adds this to the text. (By the way, do you see the word *kipper* as *kapper* in the second Hebrew morphology? That's why the translation should be "atone" not "forgive" as in NASB. There is a difference in the way *we* think of the words).

Why would the NIV *add* this temporal modifier? It's obvious. The translators of the NIV want their readers to think that there is a *separation* between covenant and atonement. The *Old Testament* covenant came first. The *New Testament* atonement came later. Full forgiveness is accomplished only *after* the New Testament atonement. In other

154

words, the NIV translation supports the idea that atonement occurs in the death of Yeshua on the cross, not in the action of YHWH when the covenant is established. Now you can appreciate why I refer to the NIV as the Nearly Inspired Version. In my view, the NIV cannot be trusted as an accurate, unbiased translation of the original text. Its theological agenda constantly shows up in the choice of vocabulary and the manipulation of the text. I hate to say this, but if there were ever a more disguised attempt to steer believers away from the truth of Scripture, I couldn't think of a better way to do it.

Now let's answer the two opening questions. When was Israel forgiven? The second God established His covenant with them. When was that? A *long time* before the cross. When were you forgiven? The moment Yeshua laid down His life on the altar in the heavenly temple. When was that? Before the foundation of the world. Israel didn't have to wait for the cross to come near to God. Neither did you. The fact that we live *after* the event of the cross doesn't change the means by which we come into fellowship with the Father. That access was established before any human being existed. We come into fellowship the same way that Israel does – through YHWH's covenant. We might notice one other thing in this verse. YHWH offers atonement in concert with the covenant. He doesn't wait thousands of years for Pilate's decision either.

Since we have argued that the cry of dereliction from the cross is really a reference to a psalm of vindication, we must treat the potentially opposing view from another prophet, Habakkuk.

155

Your eyes are too pure to approve evil, and you can not look on wickedness with favor. Why do You look with favor on those who deal treacherously? Why are You silent when the wicked swallow up those more righteous than they? Habakkuk 1:13 NASB

Habakkuk's statement forces us to ask, "Can God look on evil?" Can He intimately engage the wicked? When the sin of the world falls on Yeshua, must God turn away? Must He withdraw because Sin is so appalling, so hideous? "We cannot doubt that St. Mark intends us to understand that the Three Hours of Darkness symbolize a real darkness in the soul of Jesus: a real consequence of being forsaken by God which finds expression in the Cry of Dereliction."[79] Really? Are you willing to take another look?

Traditionally, Christian theology agrees with Hickinbotham. God abandons Yeshua at the moment Yeshua takes Sin (capital S) on Himself. This verse from Habakkuk is often used to justify the claim. But what does the prophet really say? Does he say that God cannot look on evil because holiness prevents such a thing? Read the verse again. Notice that the NASB *adds* "with favor." The Hebrew text merely says that God cannot look on *amal*, a word that means trouble, harm, anxiety and toil. The NASB attempts to capture the *idiomatic metaphor* by adding "with favor" in order indicate that it is not logically or theologically impossible for God to *view* evil but rather that God

---

[79] J. P. Hickinbotham, *The Churchman*, lviii, p. 56.

does not *condone* evil. Given what Isaiah says in 45:7, it seems difficult to imagine that God cannot even look upon sin. Even if we read Isaiah 45:7 as a statement about natural calamity rather than moral disobedience, are we prepared to say that God must turn away from any form of rebellion? If that is true, then how did we enter into fellowship with Him?

The Hebrew expression in Habakkuk uses the verbs *nabath* and *yakol*. *Nabath* covers the range from a quick glance to a studied examination. It is the same verb used in Psalm 33:13 ("He sees all the sons of men"), clearly including the wicked whom He rewards accordingly. *Yakol* basically means "to be able, to have the capacity." It is used to describe the *sovereignty* of God. There is *nothing* He cannot do. It certainly seems that Habakkuk uses the phrase metaphorically as an expression of God's *unwillingness* to overlook evil, rather than a declaration that God is *unable* to see evil.

Furthermore, if Yeshua is the Messiah, is He only the Messiah *after* the crucifixion? Is He not the Messiah *during* the crucifixion? Is He not the Son of God, the only beloved in whom the Father finds great favor, *during* the paradigm example of obedience? How are we to split apart the seconds while He hangs on the cross so that, at one moment He is glorified; at the next He is abandoned, and then glorified again?

Doesn't the problem really come from reading the text, "My God, My God, why have you abandoned me?" as if it is a declarative statement rather than a form of ostensive definition. Put aside the theological doctrine for just a moment and ask yourself, "Does Mark really intend me to imagine that God is blind to His Son's struggle and triumph?" If you were at the cross at that moment, would you have understood His cry as a statement of abandonment, or would it point you to something else?

The idea that God abandoned Yeshua because of the enormity of Sin is the equivalent of the doctrine of *non passé peccare*, that it was *impossible* for Yeshua to sin. Both theological concepts have enormous difficulties and neither seems to fit the Jewish context of the first century.

We cannot diminish the hideousness of the crucifixion, but neither should we enlarge it. Scripture actually pays little attention to the details of the event. When it could have easily informed us of the physical agony, the pain and suffering and the humiliation, Scripture relegates those descriptions to the night in the Garden of Gethsemane. The Garden is the center of the struggle. The cross is almost an afterthought. It happened. It's terrible. But what needed to be done was already done by the time the nails were used.

If God can't look on the Sin attached to Yeshua, how can He look on us who certainly aren't blameless?

Finally, we must deal with the Levitical claims about atonement.

He shall make atonement for the holy place, because of the impurities of the sons of Israel and because of their transgressions in regard to all their sins; and thus he shall do for the tent of meeting which abides with them in the midst of their impurities. Leviticus 16:16 NASB

Are we so familiar with some religious words that we no longer understand what they mean? We can use them in sentences. We can speak of their theological significance. But are we only repeating religious acronyms? Let's take this word, atonement, as an example. What does atonement mean? Leon Morris writes, "The atonement is the crucial doctrine of the faith. Unless we are right here it matters little, or so it seems to me, what we are like elsewhere."[80] Erickson and others agree. The atonement is *the* critical point of the Christian faith. But if you ask most believers what "atonement" means, they are hard-pressed to provide a clear answer. And if they suggest something about forgiving sins or about the mercy seat or about covering our guilt with the blood, they will have enormous difficulties when it comes to a verse like this one in Leviticus.

Read the verse again. Here "atonement" isn't about forgiveness. It is about *cleaning up pollution in the Tabernacle.* The verb is *kipper.* Here it is in the Piel tense. In fact, in all the verses related to sacrifice, this verb is never in the Qal tense. It is always Piel. Why does this matter? Because in the Qal, the verb means "to wipe something *on to a surface*" but in the Piel it means "to wipe something *off of a surface.*" In other words, we often think of atonement as though God is wiping the blood of the

---

[80] Leon Morris, *The Cross in the New Testament*, p. 5.

Lamb *over* our sins so that He no longer sees them. This idea is common in the expression that the blood of Yeshua *covers* our transgressions. But when this verb is used in the context of sacrifice, it never means "covering over." It means, "cleaning away." Atonement *removes* pollution.

We wish to be in God's presence and God wishes us to be there too, but we are defiled, both ritually and morally. The Levitical sacrifices are intended to remove this defilement so we can enjoy His presence. The blood washes away the defilement we bring into the Temple. But notice that it is the Temple that is cleaned, not you and me. Our impurities and sins create the need for wiping away, but the wiping away action doesn't clean the sinner. It cleans the house of God. According to the Levitical sacrifices, blood is the cleaning solvent. Blood wipes away the pollution so that we may enter into God's presence. Blood cleans the Temple. It removes the impurity so that we can be with God. Blood does not "save" us. It does not provide us with forgiveness. It simply cleans the place where God abides.

Consider the implications for our use of the word "atonement" in contemporary Christian thought. Is atonement about forgiveness, or is it about drawing near?

Now that we have examined both the prophets and the writings and the Torah, we can turn back to those other New Testament authors who seem to speak as if forgiveness is a function of the cross event. Now we will be able to read the verses in their Hebraic context. We will discover that once the Christian theological spectacles are removed, these authors agree with our assessment.

First we have to deal with the tense problems of the Greek texts. The opening of Matthew is sufficient to treat all of these kinds of translation issues at once.

She will bear a son, and you shall call his name Jesus, for he will save his people from their sins. Matthew 1:21 ESV

Is salvation proleptic? Ah, what a great word! You might have to look it up, but just in case you don't have time, "prolepsis" means "the representation of a thing as existing before it actually does or did so." For example, the phrase "dead man walking" used to describe an inmate on death row is proleptic. The inmate isn't actually dead, but he is considered such because of his anticipated outcome.

So, we ask again. Is salvation proleptic? Are we saved at the moment we accept entrance into a restored fellowship with YHWH, or are we only considered saved because the actual condition is yet to be realized? Be careful how you answer. If you say, "Yes, of course we are saved as soon as we enter into a restored relationship with YHWH," then doesn't that imply that Abraham, Samuel, David and all the men and women who lived *before* the birth of Yeshua were saved *when they were restored to fellowship by YHWH*? And if this is true, then what makes us think that salvation wasn't available until the cross? But if you say, "No, those men and women of the Old Testament weren't saved yet because Yeshua had not died on the cross," then

161

how do you explain God's statements about counting them righteous and restored?

Objectors could offer a bi-directional salvation, that is, those who lived *before* Yeshua died on the cross were counted as "saved" but really weren't "completed" until after the death of Yeshua. Salvation had *retroactive* properties. Since we no longer live in anticipation of some godly arrangement to provide us with retroactive salvation, now we are completely saved as soon as we accept Yeshua because he has already died on the cross. That sounds plausible until we come across Yeshua's own statement to the man lowered through the roof. "Your sins are forgiven," doesn't sound like, "In a few months, after I have died and been raised from the dead, your sins will actually be forgiven but for now you can consider them forgiven." In fact, to prove his point, Yeshua restores the man to health. That doesn't strike me as *proleptic healing*.

So with this tangle of terms, what do we do with the future, active, indicative, third person, singular verb *sosei* – "he will save." Doesn't that make it seem that salvation is still in the future? Doesn't that indicate that salvation is *not yet available* because the crucifixion hasn't yet happened? We are inclined to think of this Greek verb in *Greek* terms, that is, according to the Greek *linear* view of time. But a few corrections are in order. First, of course, is that the angel didn't speak Greek to Joseph (and he didn't tell Joseph to name his son "Jesus" either). The angel spoke Hebrew and in Hebrew actions are not past, present or future. They are complete or incomplete, that is, they are either finished or they are continuing. Although controversial, Thorlief Boman's insight helps us see the essential and crucial difference between Greek and Hebrew verbal forms. Hebrew verbs basically express movement or activity, as opposed to Greek verbs which express states of being. So the Greek future tense expresses a yet-to-occur state of being (salvation is yet to occur – he *will* save) while Hebrew expresses the idea as a movement not fully complete (salvation already exists but its fullest sense is on the way to being revealed). When we read the Greek verb translated into English, we attached to the action the same static states of being associated with Greek thought about linear time. But when we realize that this sentence is really Hebrew, then the statement is not about something *yet to come* but rather about the illuminating fullness of salvation anticipated when the action is finally finished.

In Greek, Joseph *waits* for salvation. In Hebrew, Joseph *already experiences salvation* but anticipates its full expression.

Why do we care about all this technicality? We care because if we understand the future tense Greek expressions as Hebraic, we realize that God's saving grace has been active since the beginning, but its full implications were not understood until the final act of the play – the cross and the resurrection. Guilt and the broken relationship that resulted from our defilement was anticipated and covered in the sacrifice of the Lamb before the foundation of the world, but the *consequence* of sin – death – was not finally overcome until the cross,

163

when we saw at last just how God dealt with the entire broken creation.

Why does this matter? Because if salvation is not available until after the crucifixion, then Abraham is not really reconciled to YHWH when YHWH says, "I will establish My covenant between Me and you." And we really have *two different religions!*

Now we will examine the passages in John that seem to suggest that the cross is the place of atonement.

For God did not send the Son into the world to judge the world; but that the world should be saved through Him. John 3:17 NASB

John attempts to answer the question, "Why did Yeshua come?" Most believers will say something like, "To save us from our sins," or "To forgive us so we can go to heaven." Because we are preoccupied with our own guilt, we tend to read gospel statements about His purpose as if they are exclusively about us, but if we pay close attention to the words, we find another focus. John, for example, points out that the *cosmos* is in need of deliverance, not just human beings. Paul says effectively the same thing: "the whole creation groans and suffers the pains of child-birth together until now" (Romans 8:22). While there is no question that Yeshua forgives human beings, even His own declaration about purpose does not include this fact. In conversation with Pilate, He replied, "You say correctly that I am a king. For this I have been born, and for this I have come into the world, to bear witness to the truth" (John 18:37). Not a word about forgiveness, sin or guilt; rather, a bold statement about ushering in the Kingdom on earth. Perhaps we are simply sin-myopic. We see it everywhere so it overtakes our appreciation of the much bigger picture, that is, *all creation* needs salvation.

If we realize that atonement is not "at-one-ment" with God *for us*, but rather the removal of defilement that prevents the presence of God among His creation, then we may perhaps see that the purpose of the incarnation was not to provide us access to the Father. That was already in place from the time of Adam, and, in fact, was a consistent experience of men and women since the time of Adam. Human beings were not barred from God because of sin. Forgiveness was available since before the foundation. But God's presence in and throughout the earth was barred because of the *consequences* of disobedience, both human and angelic. In other words, the God of life did not enjoy full presence in His creation because the creation contained the presence of death, the penalty for disobedience. Atonement was required to *wipe away* this defilement in order that God and His creation, *all of His creation*, could be joined again in perfect harmony. Back to the Garden, my friends, back to the Garden.

Now, if atonement is the wiping away of what defiles so that God and creation are reunited, then Yeshua's death takes on cosmic proportions. Through death, God conquers death, and as a result, the defilement of death is removed from all creation. God Himself executes the plan of *full* redemption. That plan includes us, of course, but we are not the single focus of this monumental victory. We may have been the cause (perhaps), but we are not the only players in this game. You will recall that the pollution of sin once before affected the entire earth and it was necessary for God to even *wipe away* the vegetation in the Flood. Why? Do plants sin? While plants have no moral consciousness, they are apparently subject to the corruption brought about by the sins of men. The *earth itself* is caught up in the abomination of disobedience. So the Flood comes to *clean* even the earth. Temporarily. Death still remained and until death was removed, the entire cosmos was defiled. The *permanent* solution to removing this defilement was the cross and the resurrection.

So atonement cleans. It cleans the place that has been defiled so that God may enter and His presence will become a reality. Atonement *washes away* what prevents God's presence; and that must mean that atonement has to deal with death.

"That the world might be saved." *Kosmos sothe* – from the Greek verb *sozo*. But here the verb is aorist, passive, subjunctive. The saving action happens to the world. The active agent is someone else – the Son. And when it occurs (subjunctive), it is all over with – aorist – a completed action in the past. The deliverance of the world doesn't have to be repeated again and again. Once this atonement is accomplished, nothing more needs to be done – ever.

That sounds like two other statements in the New Testament. "It is accomplished," (John 19:30) and "and not through the blood of goats and calves, but through His own blood, He entered the holy place once for all, having obtained eternal redemption" (Hebrews 9:12).

"And for their sake I consecrate myself, that they also may be sanctified in truth." John 17:19 ESV

"The language is equally appropriate to the preparation of a priest and the preparation of a sacrifice; it is therefore doubly appropriate to Christ."[81] Barrett's comment about the Greek word *hagiazo* ("consecrate") is now so commonplace that we hardly register any question about it. Erickson nods approvingly when he notes that the verb *hagiazo* is "a term common in sacrificial contexts."[82] "His death was a *sacrifice* typified by the Old Testament sacrificial system."[83] We could quote many others. Everyone seems to recognize that Yeshua speaks about His death in Old Testament sacrificial terms. But then how is it possible to ignore that fact that His death does *not* meet the requirements of an Old Testament sacrifice? Are we so intent on fitting the death of Yeshua into our Christian paradigm that we are willing to overlook its complete *misfit* with everything about a sacrifice that any Jew would have known? The Christian theologians are right. Yeshua's death is described as an atoning sacrifice. But it certainly doesn't fit the Levitical system. If it is a sacrifice, it must be a sacrifice of another order.

---

[81] C. K. Barrett, *The Gospel According to St. John*, 2nd Edition (Westminster, 1978), p. 571.
[82] Millard Erickson, *Christian Theology* (1st Edition), p. 807.
[83] *Ibid.*, p. 808.

167

It's worth noting that this verb (*hagiazo*) is used twice in Yeshua's statement. It is the same verb translated "may be sanctified." Yeshua consecrates himself in order that his disciples may be consecrated, or He sanctifies Himself so that they may be sanctified. Recognizing that the action is the same for both parties helps us remove the idea that Yeshua does something radically different than what is expected of his disciples. What He does is also something that they will do.

But this means that Yeshua cannot have the *cross* in mind because He is not expecting all His disciples to also be crucified as sacrifices for sin. *Hagiazo* is about entering into a state of holiness (cf. Isaiah 5:16, Ezekiel 36:23, Exodus 19:10). It is an act of *dedication* to God's absolute standard of holiness. The etymology of the word makes it clear that it is to be understood within the framework of religious practice and ritual. In rabbinic Judaism, this word is used to describe those who keep Torah and who separate themselves from pagan practices. Paul's use of the term helps us see what Yeshua intends. In Romans 12:1, Paul uses the noun form (*hagios*) to describe the believer as a "living sacrifice, holy and acceptable to God." Yeshua must mean that His disciples are to be separated, set aside for God, living examples of perfect practice within the religious community. They don't need to die on the cross, but they do need to die to self.

Here's the point for our present inquiry: the focus of Yeshua's own remark and the use of the word in both the Tanakh and the apostolic writings, is on *death*, not forgiveness. The emphasis is on the *violent separation from worldly ways*, a process

168

akin to dying. The point is the *death* of the sacrifice. We may recognize that Yeshua's death had different effects and implications than the "consecration" of His disciples, but the point is that in this final hour of prayer, Yeshua doesn't speak of dying for the forgiveness of the world's sin. He speaks of dying as a process that brings about holiness. And since He clearly intends His disciples to go through this process, it hardly seems possible to read the text as if He expected everyone who followed Him to literally be nailed to a cross. What Yeshua has in mind must be consistent with the ritual practice found in the Tanakh, perhaps deepened, perhaps extended, but certainly not incompatible, otherwise no Jew of His time would have understood how *hagiazo* could be connected to the cult (the religious practice).

What does this mean for us? It means that Yeshua expects us to be *hagios*, holy. But that word doesn't stand on its own. To be holy is to be in conformity with the holy God – and for the audiences of Yeshua, Paul, Peter and John, that means to reach the standard of the Tanakh, to be obedient to its teachings. Yeshua consecrated Himself in order for us to be able to do the same. He acted as priest. He brought His followers into the presence of the Holy God, He interceded – with the intention that they might also become holy.

Having satisfied ourselves with an examination of John's gospel, and finding it compatible with John's claim concerning the Lamb "slain before the foundation of the world," we must now examine the final two New Testament authors who deal with this subject. Perhaps the most voluminous is the author of Hebrews. Several passages are used by Christian apologists to support the forgiveness-cross connection.

For you have need of endurance, so that when you have done the will of God, you may receive what was promised. Hebrews 10:36 NASB

The Greek text actually doesn't say, "what was promised." It says, "the promise." It's not obvious why the translators decided to change a perfectly intelligible Greek word (*ten epangelian*) from a definite noun into a subjunctive clause (ESV does the same, NIV turns it into a verb). In Greek, the author of Hebrews makes it quite clear. "The promise" will be ours if and when we have done the will of God.

What is "the promise"? Well, we only have to back up a few verses to find the answer. It is the confidence to "enter the holy place," drawing near because we have had our hearts "sprinkled" and our bodies "washed" (verse 22). All of this language is taken directly from the vocabulary of ritual and moral purity found in the Tanakh. This suggests that the promise is our ability to enter into God's presence, to share fellowship with Him; and while it is certain that there is an eschatological element in this (that the *full* fellowship with the Father will one day become a reality), it is also certain that we have already been invited into this fellowship even now. Once again we discover that the author of Hebrews sees our situation as "already – but not yet."

But there is another factor at play here, one that we might skip over because of its implications. The point of this verse is to encourage *endurance*. The promise is the result of *continuing in God's will*. It isn't a "once and for all" decision. Commensurate with the approach of the Tanakh, fellowship with God requires *hesed*, and *hesed* demands faithful loyalty over time. "You *may receive*" is a subjunctive, aorist, middle, plural verb. In other words, it has significant consequence for the subject (middle); it is for all of us (plural); it is an accomplished fact (aorist); but it *depends on the condition described* (subjunctive). God pays on commission, not salary! The bonus is earned through obedience to His will. It is not guaranteed just because you signed up as an employee. Fellowship is the result of patient fortitude and persistent tenacity in the pursuit of His will; and to the victor belong the spoils.

Perhaps the NASB, NIV and ESV changed the words for "the promise" because they didn't want readers to think that the experience of fellowship with God could be judged by our *current* apprehension of His presence. Perhaps they wanted us to think that it is all far off so that we won't ask, "Am I in harmony with Him today?" It's much easier to imagine that it will all work out in the end if we don't have any standard to judge our behavior right now; but the author of Hebrews would hardly agree.

Therefore, when He comes into the world, He says, 'Sacrifice and offering Thou hast not desired, but a body Thou hast prepared for Me;'" Hebrews 10:5 NASB

171

This verse from Hebrews certainly seems as if there is a direct connection between Yeshua's entry into the world in bodily form and the preparation of an atoning sacrifice; but New Testament authors often rearrange God's word from the Tanakh in order to make some point in their own writings. Sometimes they offer rather creative translations (see, for example, my discussion of the many examples in Matthew[84]). Sometimes they combine diverse texts in order to make a new concept (even Yeshua does this). And sometimes they *change* the words entirely. Such is the case with this verse. The citation is from Psalm 40:6, but the Hebrew doesn't use the word "body" at all. In fact, not even the standard LXX text has *soma* instead of *otia* (ears). Guthrie remarks, "Although it is true that LXX B S A have *soma*, these probably should be read as corrections by scribes wishing to bring the manuscripts in line with Hebrews' quotation."[85] In other words, the author of Hebrews *altered* the verse in the Tanakh by changing "ears" to "body" and subsequent Christian copyists of the LXX changed the LXX to match the letter to the Hebrews. The verse in Psalms clearly *does not use "body."* The author of Hebrews changes the verse to fit the argument (and this is only one of four changes in this short sequences of citations).

Does this concern you? If you believe that the New Testament is inspired by the same God, and that it is an accurate record of God's infallible and inerrant truth, then this presents a real problem. How can

---

[84] http://skipmoen.com/products/hermeneutics/
[85] George Guthrie, "Hebrews" in *Commentary on the New Testament Use of the Old Testament* (eds. Beale and Carson), p. 977.

the author of Hebrews play fast and loose with the Tanakh, and claim that he is citing holy Scripture? If he can do this here, how do we know *any* of the rest of it isn't also whatever he made up along the way? How can we claim that God's truth is *one* if the authors of the Bible freely change the words whenever they wish? These are not trivial questions. They shake the foundation of our faith in the text.

What we must realize, and come to terms with, is that the authors of the New Testament documents treat the Tanakh *as Jews*, not Greeks. In our world, the Greek world, word-for-word accuracy is the definition of "citation." When we say, "This is what the Bible says," we can't imagine that we can freely change the words. Accuracy means getting the words right. But in Jewish thought, citation is the invitation to *meaning*, not words. So Jewish use of the Tanakh is open to explanations of *additional meanings*. It is not limited to exactly the same words. The author of Hebrews is no different than Paul or Matthew or John. He simply changes the words of the Tanakh in order to reveal *another meaning* of his reading of the text. That does not mean that the Hebrew word *ozen* (ear) can also mean *soma* (body). What it means is that the author of Hebrews saw in this verse in the Psalms a *connection* to another idea, and he simply incorporated that idea into the verse in Psalms. His view of inspiration, infallibility and inerrancy is radically different than ours. The author of Hebrews has a revelation. The verse in Psalms can be used to speak about the preparation of the Son as the acceptable sacrifice for sin. So he just rearranges the furniture to show that. No big deal.

He is providing a *midrash* on the text. The reason he doesn't have to tell us that it is a *midrash* is because *everyone knew what he was doing from a Jewish perspective*. Only Greeks find this suspect.

What does this mean for us? First, it tells us that the meaning of Psalm 40:6 *does not change*. It still isn't about Yeshua's body. But the author of Hebrews wants us to see Psalm 40:6 in a different way. For him, it is about the Messiah and the sacrifice – the one true sacrifice that makes all other sin offerings pale by comparison. So when you read Hebrews, remember what is happening. You are reading *interpretations* of the Tanakh, and you need to have a Hebrew mind to understand them.

Once we see what the author of Hebrews is actually doing, we recognize that the citation (?) from Psalms is not necessarily a Messianic prophecy. It is only a Messianic prophecy with the alteration provided by this author. It is prophecy *after the fact*. Therefore, the use of *soma* does not give us grounds for claiming that this *must be about the cross*. Not only is the cross not specifically mentioned, the entire statement is polemic. It serves the author's purpose and that purpose is not about forgiveness. The author of Hebrews is not self-contradictory. He claims that atonement took place in a Tabernacle not made with human hands and not of this earth, and this verse does not say otherwise.

Now we know that the word "body" is substituted for "ear" by this author. Why? Guthrie provides the following explanation: "the author appropriates the psalm as being explicitly fulfilled by Christ

174

'when he comes into the world' (10:5). This language is distinct from that used as an introductory formula in 1:6, where the author employs *oikoumene* ('world'), which can be interpreted as a reference to the heavenly realm. The use of *kosmos* ('world'), along with the context, suggests here that the incarnation is in mind (Lane 1991: 2:262-63). The psalm presents the posture of obedience and resolute intention to die on the cross, embraced by Christ in the incarnation."[86]

Sounds good, doesn't it? I have some problem with Guthrie's suggestion that *oikoumene* can be interpreted as the heavenly realm since Kittel shows that this word means "the inhabited world," and its root, *oiko*, is always connected to something about a dwelling, but the idea that the author of Hebrews employs Psalm 40:6 in order to suggest a connection to the incarnation is appealing. Does this mean that the author of Hebrews explicitly tells us that Yeshua died on the cross for the forgiveness of sin?

Consider the context. The sacrifice of bulls and goats will not take away sins (verse 4). Yeshua comes into the world (*kosmos*) to fulfill the will of the Father (verses 5-7). Sacrifices and whole burnt offerings for sin are neither effective nor desired by God (verse 8). Yeshua's sacrifice removes the need for sin sacrifices by the Levitical priesthood (verse 9). We are sanctified through the offering of the body of Yeshua HaMashiach once for all (verse 10).

---

[86] George Guthrie, "Hebrews" in *Commentary on the New Testament Use of the Old Testament* (eds. Beale and Carson), p. 977.

Note Stern's comment: "it is not necessary to suppose that this 'taking away' prohibits all animal sacrifices by the Levitical priesthood. The author's point relates to only the sin offering . . . because the second sin offering system is effectual in a way that the first never was. . . The other animal sacrifices and the Levitical priesthood could be continued without eclipsing the preeminent role of Yeshua's once-for-all sacrifice and eternal high-priesthood."[87] Stern clears up the idea that *all* sacrifices are now unnecessary. We are talking about sacrifices for sin, and in particular, deliberate sin, the real problem for the Levitical system. But what about the cross? Does any of this *demand* that the sin sacrifice be limited to the execution on the cross? That issue turns on the meaning of the word *kosmos*. Guthrie's suggestion about *kosmos* is, in fact, exactly backwards. The use of *kosmos* in the LXX includes the heavenly realm. Kittel says, "The adoption of the term *kósmos* by the LXX is an important event in its history, for this makes of it a biblical, as well as a philosophical, concept. The LXX uses *kósmos* for (a) the 'host (of heaven)' (cf. Gen. 2:1; Dt. 4:19), thus combining such ideas as order, adornment, world, heaven, and stars; (b) 'adornment' as the equivalent of various Hebrew terms, as in Ex. 33:5; Prov. 20:29; Is. 3:24; Nah. 2:10; (c) 'adornment' with no Hebrew equivalent, as in Is. 49:18; Prov. 28:17; Sir. 6:30, etc.; 1 Macc.

---

[87] David Stern, *Jewish New Testament Commentary*, p. 704.

1:22; 2:11; (d) 'universe,' substituting it in such books as Wisdom and Maccabees for the older term 'heaven and earth.'"[88] In other words, there is no linguistic reason to suggest that the sacrifice associated with Yeshua HaMashiach occurred on the cross. All this text says is that Yeshua entered the *kosmos* in bodily form in order to do the will of the Father; and since Christian theology teaches that Yeshua existed in bodily form as the Angel of the Lord in the Tanakh, there is little reason to suppose that He could not have accomplished the sacrifice for sin on the heavenly altar in bodily form.

What does the author of Hebrews want us to understand about all this? First, he wants us to know that Yeshua's sacrifice removes the problem of sin and its defilement. Secondly, he wants us to know that Yeshua's sacrifice is once-for-all (clearly it must also be applied to Abraham, Moses and the others). Thirdly, he wants us to know that Yeshua's sacrifice replaces the temporary covering provided by the Levitical rituals *on this issue*. And finally, he wants us to know that we can be assured of all this because of the fact of his death and resurrection. None of this means that God waited until the crucifixion to provide atonement for sin.

Let's examine another passage in Hebrews.

Otherwise, He would have needed to suffer often since the foundation of the world; but now once at the consummation of the ages He has been

---

[88] Kittel, G., Friedrich, G., & Bromiley, G. W. (1985). *Theological Dictionary of the New Testament* (461–462). Grand Rapids, MI: W.B. Eerdmans.

manifested to put away sin by the sacrifice of Himself. Hebrews 9:26 NASB

Exegesis of this verse depends on its context. Verse 24 reads, "For Christ did not enter a holy place made with hands . . . but into heaven itself." That seems pretty clear, doesn't it? The Messiah appears in the presence of YHWH in heaven, not on earth, to perform the heavenly sacrifice (v. 23). If this is true, then why does the author suddenly write as if the Messiah has been manifested at the consummation of the ages? That makes it seem as if the sacrifice occurs at the *end*, not the beginning. Something seems confused.

Let's start with the Greek word *synteleia* (translated "consummation"). This word is made up of two Greek words, *syn* and *teleo*. *Syn* means "in union with," or "together with," but with emphasis on the unity of the relation rather than simply proximity (as indicated by *meta*). *Teleo* is not simply the "end" of something but rather the completion, fulfillment, accomplishment or goal. This seems clear from Paul's use of *teleo* in his description of the "end of the Law," a phrase that is much better translated as "the *goal* of the Law." The author of Hebrews combines these two ideas to produce *synteleia*. This is not simply the "end." It is a special kind of end, an end of full completion and union. In the author's thought, this event fulfills an entire age, whatever that may be. Furthermore, this event occurs only once (*hapax*), never to be repeated.

So which is it? Does the sacrifice occur before the foundation of the world in the heavenly Temple not made with human hands, or does it occur once at the fulfillment of the age manifested to us? Maybe our question is correct. Maybe it's *both*! It seems quite clear from two other authors that the Lamb was slain before the foundation of the world. It also seems clear that atonement is accomplished in only *one* way and that forgiveness was available *before* the crucifixion. These facts support the statement in verse 23 that the crucial sacrifice takes place in the heavenlies. But it is still possible that the *manifestation* of this event, that is, our understanding and appreciation of it, occurs *once* at the fulfillment of the age. In other words, the reality of atonement was in place from the beginning, but our apprehension of that reality wasn't clear until we saw its manifestation in the crucifixion. The Messiah entered the tabernacle not made with human hands and accomplished what no earthly priest could (v. 11).

The author of Hebrews contrasts this manifestation with the repeated sacrifices of the earthly priests. His emphasis is on the *one time* nature of the Messiah's sacrifice; but he makes note of the necessity of *blood* spilled for this new covenant, citing the Torah's declaration "without shedding of blood there is no forgiveness." But the crucifixion does not meet this requirement, so the author must have something else in mind. What he has in mind is the *contrast* between the repeated sacrifices of the priests and the "once for all" sacrifice of the Messiah. The death on the cross is the visible manifestation of the reality of this one time sacrifice.

This requires a further note. The Greek word translated "manifested" is *pephanerotai*. It is the perfect passive indicative of the root *phaneroo*. It means "to make visible," but as a perfect passive it has the sense of someone else making something visible to us in such a way that we understand what has already happened has continuing importance in the present. In other words, the crucial event has already occurred but we are now seeing it for its true *and continuing* meaning. With regard to the timing of the crucial event, the verb is ambiguous. All it suggests is that the event *now manifest* occurred sometime prior to the manifestation. It does not imply that the event and the act of making the event visible are simultaneous. With this clarity, it is quite possible that the author of the text means to say that the event that he has already temporally located in the heavenly tabernacle before the foundation of the world is subsequently revealed to us in its earthly manifestation. It does not follow that the earthly manifestation *is* the heavenly tabernacle sacrifice.

Is this clarity or further confusion? Actually, it might be a bit of both. Hebrews is a challenging book but it cannot be read apart from a Jewish perspective of the whole New Testament. For any part to make sense, it must all make sense. And making sense of the whole is the function of a paradigm. I guess we're back at big picture issues again, aren't we?

Finally we come to the most serious of all objections to our argument, a passage in Peter's first letter that appears to *directly* tie the action of the crucifixion with the forgiveness of sins. The passage is complicated because it cites the prophet Isaiah as its authority, so we will have to look at both Peter's claims and the text from the prophet. We start with some analysis of Peter's statements, recognizing that in the same letter Peter says, "For He was foreknown before the foundation of the world, but has appeared in these last times for the sake of you" (1 Peter 1:20). Apologists argue that Peter's claim about foreknowledge does *not* entail the actual performance of the atoning event. It only requires that God knows *in advance* that such an event will occur. Of course, we have already dealt with the implications of this implied predestination (see our discussion on Psalm 139:16), but we must still show that Peter's claim about the cross does not stand in utter contradiction to his claims about the activity of God before the foundation of the world.

The verse in question is:

He himself bore our sins in his body on the tree, that we might die to sin and live to righteousness. By his wounds you have been healed. 1 Peter 2:24 ESV

This verse certainly looks like it settles the issue. Jesus bore our sins on the cross (tree) for forgiveness. What else could Peter have meant! All the concern about a literal reading of Revelation 13:8 evaporates. The sacrifice of the Lamb didn't actually occur before the foundation of the world – at least not physically. God might have had the divine *intention*, but it wasn't manifested until the cross. Even Peter's statement in the *same* letter (1 Peter 1:20) will have to be understood as *intention*, not execution.

181

However, if Yeshua really wanted Nicodemus to understand the cross as God's final act of forgiveness, then why did He point to the *serpent* on the pole? Wouldn't it have made more sense to point to the *pole*? And since the cross was an unmistakable symbol of *pagan power* and a complete offense to the Jews, how can we explain its supposed appearance as a substitute for the altar where God's protocol for redemption was crystal clear? When Paul says that the cross is a stumbling block to the Jews (1 Corinthians 1:23), does he mean that it causes offense because it *replaces* the altar or does he mean that it causes offense because it is incompatible with the customary expectations of the Messiah? The answer depends on additional exegetical work since either view could explain Paul's statement. Peter is a more difficult case. Here he seems to directly and unequivocally equate forgiveness with the cross, since the Greek word *xylon* is the New Testament word for "cross." Literally, the word means "wood," in particular "dry wood as opposed to living, green wood." That the word is used with reference to the cross is clear from Acts 5:30 and 10:39, although in Revelation 2:7 and 22:2 it is used for the "tree" of life – but certainly Peter has the cross, the dead wooden stake, in mind.

How are we to resolve this? We must begin with the context. Peter acknowledges his readers as "aliens and strangers," urging them to live in such a manner that their contemporaries have nothing to say but praise for God. He continues with a list of actions that will insure recognition of God's saving work in their lives because they display observable, peaceable behavior regardless of the circumstances. Peter notes that this may mean suffering without justification, but he commends these actions because they model the same actions and attitude taken by Yeshua. The Messiah's prior affliction is an "example for you to follow in His steps" (1 Peter 2:21).

Then Peter provides the lynchpin of his exhortation. He uses a rabbinic technique called *kal va-chomer* (light to heavy). If Yeshua was reviled and mistreated and yet did not respond in like manner, if He lived as a man without sin and yet was judged unfairly, *if He bore our sins in His body on the cross*, how much more ought we to endure what we suffer on His behalf. After all, we are not sinless. We are not completely trusting. We cannot save others. And yet we are called to be like Him in all these things. The context shows us that the statement about bearing sins in His body on the cross comes in the middle of an argument about living as a witness to God regardless of our circumstances. In other words, Peter is not attempting to give his readers a theology of the cross. He is using the cross as the symbol of final injustice and humiliation endured by the Messiah and, therefore, a call to us to endure our circumstances of injustice and humiliation in order to glorify God. Peter's purpose is to establish a standard of enduring trust under extreme circumstances. He does this by pointing to the actions of Yeshua, ultimately culminating in the crucifixion. The whole argument is not about being saved. It is about enduring faithfulness in order to glorify God. The paradigm case of unjust suffering is the death of the Messiah by crucifixion, a death that was endured without complaint. In fact, it was the sinful acts of men such as ourselves who brought about this tragic injustice. Therefore, if Yeshua can endure the agony of crucifixion unjustly without loss of trust in God, *how much more* are we expected to endure the lesser suffering in our lives to God's glory?

This doesn't resolve the forgiveness issue, but at least it clarifies Peter's motivation. It prevents us from thinking that Peter simply endorses our post-Augustinian view of the cross. But more needs to be done.

Despite our examination of Peter's motivation, that is, endurance in suffering, the claim that Yeshua died on the cross for the forgiveness of sins seems clear enough. Even if Peter uses it as an example of suffering, he still seems to claim that sins were an integral part of the crucifixion. But now we need to take a step back. We need to take off our already-formed Christian doctrinal hats and see if we can view this claim within mindset of the first century Gentile followers of the Way, followers who did *not* come to the Scriptures with 2000 years of cultural Christianity. In fact, since Peter is writing to an audience that included Gentiles, we can't even claim that his audience had a *Jewish perspective.*

Let's consider the audience once more. Certainly they have some familiarity with the Tanakh. If they didn't, Peter's citations as authority for his arguments would mean nothing; but look at the argument Peter provides. To these Gentiles he says, "You are a chosen race, a royal priesthood" clearly citing Deuteronomy 10:15. Then he calls his readers who were once "not a people," now "the people of God," employing Hosea. His argument about endurance relies heavily on Isaiah's portrait of the suffering servant. What does Peter accomplish with these references in the Tanakh? He clearly means to include the Gentiles in the commonwealth of Israel. He wants them to know they are grafted in. How will they know that these statements from the Tanakh apply to them? Not by consulting the text since it is clear from the text that the statements Peter cites are intended for *Jews*, not Gentiles. Peter must construct a midrash, the application of a text from one set of circumstances to a different set of circumstances. When Peter *applies* these texts to the Gentiles, he accomplishes two things. First, he informs these Gentiles that they have *equal standing* in the Kingdom. This is particularly important given Peter's previous hypocrisy about Gentiles. Secondly, Peter's citations demonstrate that the claims of detractors who expected Gentiles to enter as proselytes are false. What God accepts, men may not reject (the lesson of Peter's vision on the rooftop).

The technique of midrash doesn't stop with verse 23. Our inquiry into verse 24 is also part of the midrash. But now we need to have a better understanding of midrash itself. There are two kinds of midrashim. The first is midrash aggadah – a midrash that explains some biblical passage by adding a story to the passage. One of the best examples of this kind of midrash is the story about Abram smashing the idols in his father's house before God called him out of Mesopotamia. The story is merely a legend, but it is a useful legend because it supplies background about Abram's character in order for us to understand his response to God's call. Midrash aggadah focuses on character, values, ethics and ideas that answer implicit questions posed by the text (like, "Why did Abram immediately leave Ur when God called?").

The second kind of midrash is midrash halachah. This kind of midrash attempts to explain some passage of Scripture by elucidating what it means in practice. While aggadah is not binding on the community, halachah is. If the midrash halachah about work on the Sabbath explains what it means to carry an object to the Temple, then that explanation becomes the code of conduct for the worshipping community.

Which kind of midrash is Peter employing? Is he providing an explanatory story in order to give us non-biblical background? No, he is providing binding community exegesis and application. This is midrash halachah and it concerns the status and role of Gentiles in the Messianic community. What is the final point in Peter's argument that the Gentiles have equal status and a God-given role to play? Yeshua died for them too. He bore their sins on the tree. That allusion takes us back to Isaiah (which also establishes Peter's claim that the Gentiles have always had a place in the Kingdom). We must know what Isaiah says in order to understand what Peter says.

Lancaster and Monson wrote an extended analysis of the Isaiah passage, comparing it to the oldest known copy found in Qumran (1QIsa 44:1-22). As a result of this study, they propose revisions to the much later Masoretic text. In particular, they find that Isaiah's prophecy *as known in the first century* has some significant differences from the text used in standard translations of English Bibles. Isaiah 53:5-6 are crucial for our understanding of Peter's midrash. According to 1QIsa, the text of Isaiah reads,

In reality, however, he bore our sicknesses, and our pains – he carried them. And us? We regarded him as plagued, and struck down by God and humbled. But he, yes he, is being defiled from our transgressions and is being crushed from our iniquities; even the punishment which makes our wholeness – it was upon him! And because of the bruising blows he received – healing is ours![89]

If you compare this translation with the usual English Bible translations, you will see a great deal of similarity, but also some striking differences. Nevertheless, there is certainly enough in common for Peter to *apply* this passage to the events surrounding the crucifixion. But notice what is *not* in this Isaiah text. There is no mention at all of a cross, a stake or a pole. Peter applies the Isaiah passage to the cross because he recognizes similarities and those similarities serve his purpose, namely, to show that suffering has spiritual value for Jew and Gentile alike. In other words, Peter's intention is to use the paradigm case of Yeshua's suffering as a demonstration that obedience leads to God's glory, even in affliction. The cross is the symbol of intense suffering, so Peter employs that symbol to make his point. He draws on the Isaiah

---

[89] Steven Lancaster and James Monson, *Isaiah's Exalted Servant in the Great Isaiah Scroll*, First Fruits of Zion, Issue 107, Spring 2011, p. 8.

passage to show that there is a foundation in the Tanakh for this principle. Spiritual value is acquired even in this most hideous example of the power of a pagan empire. Peter adds "on the tree [cross]" to the Isaiah text in order to set the standard of righteous suffering. He alters the Isaiah text to fit his purposes.

This forces us to consider the Isaiah passage. When we look carefully, we find more clues about Peter's alteration of the citation. We are dealing with translation differences, midrash and motivation. Peter translates this passage from Isaiah as *hos tas hamartias hemon autos anenenken* ("He Himself bore our sins"). You will immediately see that Peter changes Isaiah's word, *hola-yenu* (our griefs, our sicknesses) to *hamartias hemon* (our sins). The context and meaning in Isaiah is crucial here. The usual translation of Isaiah's proclamation is "sicknesses," derived from the verb *hala* (to become sick, weak, diseased, grieved). What we must notice is that *hola-yenu* is **not** about the *guilt* of our disobedience. It is about the *consequences* of our disobedience. The servant in Isaiah bears the *consequences* of sin. Isaiah does *not* use any of the usual Hebrew words for sin. His focus is not on disobedience, but rather on the *results* of disobedience. Just as sickness is not the *cause* but rather the symptom, so the consequences of sin are not the cause but the symptom. The consequence of sin is death, but death is not the cause of sin. Isaiah's suffering servant bears the *consequences* in this prophetic description of the cross.

John and Peter both suggest that the guilt that results in these consequences was dealt with before

188

the foundation of the world. The symptom of death still had to be dealt with – and that is accomplished on the cross. The fact that Peter reaches back to the Isaiah passage makes it clear that Peter has the *consequences* in mind, not the guilt that caused those consequences. In other words, Peter is saying that Yeshua bore the *hola-yenu* on the cross, perfectly in line with his own declaration that the guilt sacrifice, not the consequence correction, occurred before God formed the world.

But if this is the case, why does Peter use the word *hamartias* (sins) rather than the proper Greek word for grief, *penthos*. A quick examination of the meaning of *penthos* provides the answer. In classical Greek as well as New Testament Greek, *penthos* is an emotional state typically associated with mourning the dead. It is used in the LXX for prophecies of disaster and judgment. Its closer translation would be "lament" associated with shame and unrepentant sin. As we see, most of these contexts are extremely negative, more in line with funeral dirges than restoration of the Kingdom of Heaven. In fact, even the positive use of *penthountes* (Matthew 5:4) is eschatological, recovering joy *after present suffering.* Clearly Peter does not wish to portray his exhortation for endurance as though it were connected to feelings at a funeral. Peter wants his readers to see the *triumph* and *perseverance* that produces glory. Therefore, he is forced linguistically to follow the LXX translation of Isaiah 53:4 (*hotos tas hamartias hemon*). There is no doubt that Peter's motivation is to provide the paradigm case of unjust suffering as exhortation to his current readers, but since those readers include Greek-speaking Gentiles, this paradigm is enhanced by pointing to the most humiliating and shameful execution known in the Roman Empire. It is significant that neither the MT nor the LXX contains the words "on the tree." This is Peter's *addition* in order to make the midrash applicable to his purpose – enduring suffering that leads to glorification.

What conclusion can we draw about Peter's declaration that Yeshua bore our sins on the cross? Deeper analysis shows that Peter's motivation is not soteriological and neither are his references to the Tanakh. "On the cross" is a paradigm event-locator, not necessarily a theological statement about the place of atonement.

Since we cannot ask Peter to explain his thinking, we are left with only speculative alternatives. We must read Peter within the larger context of other New Testament and Old Testament passages; and that means that this verse in Peter, perhaps the *strongest* case against an understanding of the sacrificial atonement before the foundation of the It is likely that Peter added the words, "on the cross" because they enhanced his purpose, not because they told his reader *where* forgiveness occurred.

If we believe that atonement takes place "before the foundation of the world," and *not on the cross*, what doesn't change? Yeshua is still our sacrificial, substitutionary atonement. God still deals with sin in His plan of restoration. Death is still overcome. We are still redeemed. Unjust suffering still brings glory to God. We are still called to follow Yeshua. Sin is still forgiven.

What does change? Only the claim that the *crucifixion* was the place of atonement.

Why is this so crucial? Because if atonement occurs on the cross, then it is possible to claim that followers of YHWH prior to the cross were "saved" by some other means no longer applicable. If atonement occurs on the cross, then there is motivation for drawing a division between Jew and Christian. If atonement occurs on the cross, then the sacrificial system has ended and holy days like Yom Kippur are obsolete. If atonement occurs on the cross, then the Tabernacle and Temple are merely "shadows" of a different, replacement reality. And, of course, if the cross is the place of atonement, then the Church has a new symbol of forgiveness, one that is antithetical to everything God did with Israel.

One final verse must be considered. But this verse is not in the Protestant canon. It is found in the book of 1 Enoch. Why should be care about a statement from a non-canonical book? Because the cultural background of 1 Enoch gives us insights into the thinking of the canonical authors.

Most Christians have never heard of the Book of Enoch. Written about 300 BCE, it is a part of Jewish apocalyptic literature. Some of it is actually quoted in the canonical New Testament book of Jude (Jude 1:14-15). It is still considered canonical by the Ethiopian Orthodox Church and the Eritrean Orthodox Tewahedo Church and during the time of Yeshua it would certainly have been recognized as part of the body of Jewish literature. What makes this particularly important for our examination of the idea of Yeshua's sacrifice before the foundation of the world are the statements in Enoch 48.

And at that hour that Son of Man was named In the presence of the Lord of Spirits, and his name before the Head of Days. (1 Enoch 48:2)

All who dwell on earth shall fall down and worship before him, and will praise and bless and celebrate with song the Lord of Spirits. And for this reason hath he been chosen and hidden before Him, before the creation of the world and for evermore. (1 Enoch 48:5-6)[90]

These texts support the claim that the "Son of Man," a term of *divinity*, not humanity,[91] pre-exists the formation of the world and is worthy of worship as divine. The common phraseology applied to Yeshua by Christians is found in this *Jewish* literature. Verse 3 calls the "Son of Man" a "light of the Gentiles" or "the light of the nations." If the Son of Man in 1 Enoch is worthy of worship and a light to the nations, then he has obviously fulfilled the requirements that allow the Gentiles to approach YHWH in worship and he is himself divine. Remember that these are *Jewish* texts, written at least 200 years before Yeshua was born. Clearly some factions of Judaism were looking for the kind of Messiah that Yeshua claimed to be. It is a very short step from this literature to claim that the sacrificial work of the Messiah *also occurred* before the foundation of the world. The texts of John's

---

[90] http://www.qbible.com/enoch/48.html

[91] see the clarification of these terms in Daniel Boyarin, *The Jewish Gospels*.

apocalyptic and Peter's letter fit easily into the literature of the much earlier 1 Enoch.

This gives us further evidence that the statements in Revelation and 1 Peter are consistent with Jewish understanding of the pre-existent role of the Messiah. When John, Peter and the author of Hebrews add the fact that in his pre-existent role Yeshua entered the heavenly Tabernacle to perform the sacrifice needed for the forgiveness of sin as a priest of the order of Melchizedek, they are not saying anything that would have been unrecognizable to a Jewish audience; but to suggest that the sin sacrifice occurred *on the cross* doesn't fit any Jewish understanding of this sacrifice. Once again we are confronted with an exegetical choice. We either claim that what these men said makes sense within the context of their own reading audience, or we claim that they introduce completely novel and *unconscionable* thoughts to Jews. Given the undisputed fact that nearly all believers in Yeshua as the Messiah for the first ten years after the crucifixion were Jewish, which makes more sense?

Chapter Five

The End is the Beginning

We began this inquiry with the question, "What would a first-century Jewish follower of Yeshua think about the cross?" I believe we have answered that question. A first century Jew would see the cross as a literal and symbolic representation of the power of the Roman Empire. That power was exhibited in the Empire's ability to put someone to death by the most torturous method men could devise. For a Jew, the cross is a sign of *pagan* power and execution. No first century Jew would have ever considered the cross a place of atonement.

This answer implies several other truths about the earliest followers of Yeshua HaMashiach. First, it suggests that until the destruction of the Temple, they continued the Levitical sacrifices as directed by Torah, and recognized those sacrifices as one means of atonement. Secondly, it suggests that every Jew in the first century knew that atonement could be obtained by a wide variety of rituals and practices, not all of which required the slaughtering of an animal. Thirdly, it suggests that no Jew thought of the cross event as the demarcation between righteousness by "works" and righteousness by "grace." Every observant Jew knew that God's grace (*hen*) was initiated and accomplished by God alone and had always been so. Followers of the Way did not depart from this view in spite of their claims that Yeshua was the promised Messiah. Finally, our investigation has

194

shown that the cross is *absolutely central* to the purposes of God in the Messiah because it deals with the question of *kingdom*. That question is one of power and promise. No kingdom on earth and no human king can provide an answer for the final question of life, that is, the question about death. But Yeshua does have the answer. His answer is seen in the defeat of death on the cross. The cross is the place of the final victory of God's restoration over the defilement death causes. Guilt is a matter for atonement, and God deals with that matter through His Son "before the foundation of the earth." But death is a matter of penalty and God deals with this matter by sending His Son to conquer this last stranglehold on the creation itself. Death has lost its sting because the King of the Jews has overcome it.

In the end, the cross is at the center of the good news to the pagan world. It is not sin that causes pagans to lie awake at night, worrying about their lives. It is *death*; the inevitability of dying. Death strips away all human meaning, as Qohelet so eloquently explained. It is death that must be met and defeated. And that's why Yeshua goes to the cross.

I recently attended a funeral for a close relative. The Scripture readings were telling because none focused on forgiveness. In the face of death, human beings look for answers that provide hope. The readings from Isaiah 25, 6-9, 1 Corinthians 15:51-57 and Matthew 25:31-46 all had one theme: victory over death. Each of these readings was about the *necessity* of hope beyond the inevitability of dying. In the end, theological arguments and speculations fail us. In the end, it is the mystery of *death* that must be resolved. The Bible provides an answer to the universal human question. That answer is the establishment of a Kingdom that will never fail, never expire, never fade. And the reason it will never end is because its King will never die again. We have eternal life, not just remittance from sin, because our King lives eternally and all the citizens of His Kingdom share in His life.

This conclusion calls into question centuries of Christian doctrine, but it does not do so lightly. This conclusion seeks to be true to the ethos of the first century Jewish authors of the New Testament text. It seeks to be consistent with the writings of the Tanakh, seeing no place for the Christian idea of a division between the "old" and the "new" testaments. It destroys the doctrine that a relationship with God before Yeshua's incarnation is somehow based on a different foundation than after His crucifixion. Salvation is uniform in execution and application. Finally, this conclusion forces us to confront the implicit anti-Semitism of a doctrine that places the most potent symbol of pagan power and Jewish torture at the center of its religious icons. The very fact that Christianity is known throughout the world as the religion of the *cross* should have given us considerable grief rather than devoted adoration. Now we can appreciate the true meaning of the cross and see why it is such a powerful symbol of God's restoration purposes without suggesting that it opposes Jewish thought and practice. Now the cross has a place among Jews and is completely repositioned among Christians.

Why did Yeshua die on the cross? Because it was the coronation of the *eternal* King of power and glory. The cross sets the stage for the reconciliation of the *universe*!

Yeshua didn't die on the cross to forgive me of my sins. Yeshua died on the cross the wipe away the defilement of death and restore the Kingdom of Heaven to the cosmos.

Other books by Skip Moen are available at:

skipmoen.com

Words to Lead By

The Lucky Life

God, Time and the Limits of Omniscience

Spiritual Restoration Vols. 1-3

Jesus Said to Her

Guardian Angel

Members of the *At God's Table* worldwide
community receive a word study every day and
have access to more than 4000 studies and lectures
on the web site

Made in the USA
San Bernardino, CA
21 November 2013